UNDISCOVERED ISLANDS OF THE CARIBBEAN

BY BURL WILLES

An RDR Syndicate Production
Copyright © 1988 by RDR Syndicate
Cover and maps Copyright © 1988 by John Muir Publications

Library of Congress Catalog No. 87-043135

Published by
John Muir Publications
Santa Fe, New Mexico

Design/Production Mary Shapiro
Illustrations U.L. Costa
Maps and Cover Holly Wood
Typography Copygraphics, Inc.

ISBN 0-912528-80-X

Printed in the United States of America

Distributed to the booktrade by:
W.W. Norton & Company
New York, NY

Acknowledgement

This book would not have been possible without the expert help of gentle and intrepid traveler Derk Richardson, who researched and wrote much of it, and his beautiful and intelligent wife Robin, who charmed the local inhabitants from Holbox to Coche, and made possible the many friendly encounters and stories Derk describes so well. Thank you also to Peter Beren, Roger Rapoport, Ken Luboff, Steven Cary and the staff of John Muir Publications for their help.

TABLE OF CONTENTS

INTRODUCTION

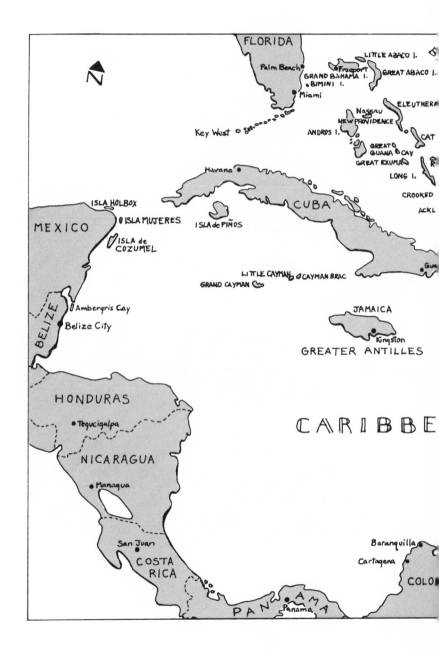

Introduction

The notion of a Caribbean vacation conjures up images of St. Thomas, Jamaica, Puerto Rico and Trinidad. There are, however, thousands of undiscovered islands in the Caribbean. Most of them are uninhabited. But between the well-known tourist spots with their time-share condos, crowded beaches and duty-free shopping and the deserted, barren cays, dozens of secluded islands await the adventurous traveler. Although one can still find beauty and tranquility on the larger and more popular islands, such islands as Saba, Marie-Galante, Culebra, and the others described herein offer an escape to a seemingly bygone era, when the Caribbean was unspoiled by highrise hotels, skyrocketing costs, ungainly crowds and traffic jams. Many of these islands are rarely visited by more than a few dozen tourists at any one time. Some are so undiscovered that inhabitants of nearby islands may not even know whether or not they are populated.

All these undiscovered islands are characterized by a quiet, unhurried lifestyle. On nearly all, reasonably-priced accommodations are available. On most, the beaches are breathtaking, and frequently empty. On many, the terrain is startling in its beauty, thick with green vegetation highlighted by brilliant blossoms. And as a rule, visitors are greeted by friendly local residents who welcome travelers into small guesthouses and charming inns. "So, you're going to reveal all these wonderful islands in your book and spoil them!" More than one friend expressed that reservation about this project. But most of these islands were selected not only because they are undiscovered, but because they are not especially vulnerable to rapid commercialization. A few require exceptional effort to reach, several have natural barriers to development, such as limited water supplies, and on others, the population has taken steps to preserve the land and wildlife from rampant exploitation.

Indeed, travelers who prefer to remain off the beaten track must be prepared to forego such conveniences of the modern world as perfect plumbing, air conditioning, television, and easy access. Such precautions as reconfirming flights, taking carry-on luggage, gathering maps, schedules and explicit directions, and watching for hidden costs such as hotel taxes and service charges will often defer the difficulties.

Encountering the unexpected is what makes traveling to these islands so special. They are not booming tourist centers, opulently endowed with luxurious amenities. But they are full of marvelous surprises, from the natural splendor of the landscape, through the enduring reminders of the region's fascinating history, down to the intimate details of gracious hospitality.

Many of the islands encourage a certain amount of tourism: their populations depend on it to bolster the local economy, and to provide employment for the members of the younger generations who might otherwise migrate to larger islands. Moreover, travelers who are respectful of local values and customs can actually make valuable contributions to the island's economy and culture. On Carriacou, for instance, Andrew Young has restored a 300-year-old stone house for rental. A few more visitors would make it possible for him to plant his dream garden.

Lest the readers fear this book has exposed the last few undiscovered islands in the Caribbean, take comfort in the knowledge that only the most intrepid travelers tend to explore most of these hideaways; and that a handful of remote islands remain secluded even from these pages. So, as I learned on Union, in the Grenadines, walk softly, do not run through these undiscovered islands.

THE BAHAMAS

GREEN TURTLE CAY, THE ABACOS

The Abacos, located just over 100 miles north of Nassau, and 200 miles northeast of Miami, are gradually outgrowing their status as "out" or Family Islands in the Bahamas. Marsh Harbor, on Great Abaco, is a developed commercial center. Walker's Cay and Treasure Cay are luxury resort areas. But Green Turtle Cay, a short ferry ride from Treasure Cay, retains much of the charm of its late 18th century origins, especially in its main settlement of New Plymouth, a storybook village with narrow streets and old New England-style clapboard buildings painted in bright whites and delicious pastels. New Plymouth provides a delightful trip back in time, while other aspects of Green Turtle Cay are perfect for the vacationer who wants to enjoy the water activities of the Bahamas without the highlife of shopping and gambling.

Like much of the Abacos, Green Turtle Cay was settled in the late 1700s by British Loyalists who exiled themselves from the United States after the Revolutionary War. Descendants of the Loyalists and their slaves are the main inhabitants of the island today, where such family names as Lowe and Sawyer are still predominant. Again in the Abaco tradition, Green Turtle was once known for its fine boat building. Pineapple farming was also a major activity. But today, the restful island depends largely on fishing, services and the small tourist trade.

New Plymouth is situated on a small peninsula with a main harbor at one end and the smaller ferry dock facing in on Black Sound. As we approached the town on the tiny Green Turtle Ferry, we could have been sailing into an old fishing village on the northeastern coast of colonial America. On every little immaculate street, hand-painted signs request "Keep GTC Clean," and people respond with a thoroughness that should leave any modern city dweller dumbfounded. A stroll through this genuinely quaint village takes you along tidy, paved streets that are essentially broad sidewalks, past the whitewashed picket fences that surround private gardens ablaze with colorful flowers, and neatly appointed houses with gaily painted dormers and gingerbread trim. Children, many of whom look very much alike because of the close family ties, ride by on bicycles. And a few tiny cars and mini-vans move slowly down the streets. The town includes several stores, a few restaurants, a fascinating museum, and a half-dozen churches representing several different denominations.

Much of the tourist trade is concentrated on White Sound, across the bay from New Plymouth, where the Green Turtle Club and Bluff House welcome the largest number of aquatically-inclined guests. From New Plymouth, it is a short ride on the Green Turtle Ferry, or a long hot walk around Black Sound. But if you walk, you can take a side trip out to the ocean side of the island for the best shelling. (Note: If you walk, be sure to ask for specific directions to wherever you are going. And ask again until you are sure, for Green Turtle's roads branch off in many directions. We walked in circles on the way to Bluff House, ending up at the back of the Green Turtle Club three different times.) Brendal's Dive Shop (Telephone: 809-367-2572) is located right on the Green Turtle Club marina, offering equipment rentals, air fills and scuba, snorkeling and picnic trips. Just beyond the two resorts, crescent-shaped Coco Bay sits with calm shallow waters in a palm-lined cove.

Activity peaks on Green Turtle on New Year's Day, when local

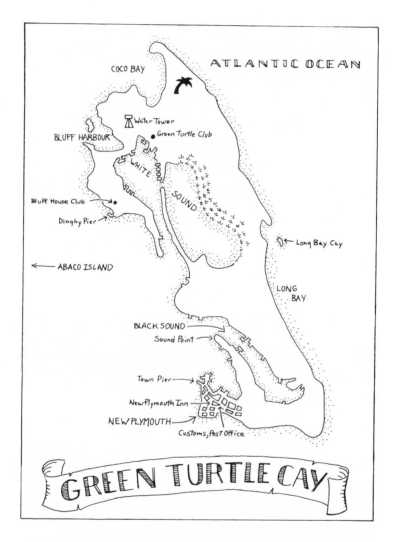

COCO BAY

ATLANTIC OCEAN

Water Tower

Green Turtle Club

BLUFF HARBOUR

WHITE SOUND

Bluff House Club

Dinghy Pier

Long Bay Cay

ABACO ISLAND

LONG BAY

BLACK SOUND

Sound Point

Town Pier

New Plymouth Inn

NEW PLYMOUTH

Customs, Post Office

GREEN TURTLE CAY

residents celebrate the capture of "Bunce," a folkloric figure who hid in Abaco's forests; in May, during the annual fishing tournament, and during the week of July 4th for the sailing regatta. But for most of the year, the sense of harmony and well-being is undisturbed on

this Bahamian Family Island. You step into a way of life that is determined not by the whims and fancies of high-rolling tourists, but by
the modest needs and traditional patterns of Green Turtle Cay's
peaceful residents.

NOTEWORTHY

MISS EMILY'S BLUE BEE BAR, in New Plymouth on Parliament
Street, is famous for the Goombay Smash, a fruity rum drink that
Miss Emily blends according to her own secret recipe. The simple
two-room bar is the most popular watering hole in New Plymouth,
and hundreds of off-islanders have left their business cards tacked
to the walls. And the ice cold Goombay Smash is as delicious and
potent as Miss Emily is charming.

THE ALBERT LOWE MUSEUM is housed in a pretty, 150-year-
old, green-trimmed white building near the New Plymouth Club
& Inn. It is owned by Alton Lowe, a renowned Abaco painter whose
work depicting the Abaco people and their way of life is featured
on the island's stamps. Exhibits include artwork, shell collections,
artifacts from the earliest days of settlement, and ship models built
by Albert Lowe.

THE LOYALIST MEMORIAL SCULPTURE GARDEN, across the
street from the New Plymouth Club & Inn, was dedicated on November 14, 1987. It features 24 bronze busts of early Loyalists, arranged
in the pattern of the Union Jack around a central pedestal with
two female figures, one white and one black. The garden is testi-
mony to the degree that this settlement reveres and stays close to
its historical roots.

ROOSTER'S REST PUB & RESTAURANT, on a low hill on the

The Bahamas

outskirts of New Plymouth, is the hot spot on weekend nights. The local band, the Gully Roosters, plays Caribbean dance music, mostly *soca* and reggae, that keeps the spacious bar jumping with a large, integrated crowd of dancers. The energy of both the band and the patrons seems boundless, but anyone needing a breather steps out on the broad deck and rests beneath a black sky studded with millions of shimmering stars.

WHERE TO STAY
NEW PLYMOUTH CLUB & INN
Telephone: (809) 367-5211
If you have arranged ahead to stay at this charming antique inn, Wally Davies will meet you at the ferry dock and transport you the two or three blocks in his electric golf cart. The eight rooms in the pink and white building are immaculate, with carpets, lace curtains, ceiling fans and antique furniture. Wally and his wife Patty are gracious, but not doting, hosts. Wally's almost shy demeanor and wry sense of humor make him an unusual and ingratiating innkeeper. He and Patty preside over meals in the tastefully decorated dining area, which has a comfortable indoor room, and a canvas-walled porch that extends towards the garden swimming pool. The dinners, featuring some elements of native cuisine, are prepared by Bahamian cooks. Rates are $100 double (plus hotel tax and service) including breakfast and dinner.

SEA STAR BEACH COTTAGES
P.O. Box 282
Gilham Bay, Green Turtle Cay, Bahamas
Telephone: (809) 367-5177
These simple beachfront cottages are tucked away in 19 acres of coconut palms, citrus and banana trees, hibiscus and bougainvillaea.

Located one-half mile from New Plymouth, by footpath, they rent for $60 for one-bedroom, $75 for a two-bedroom cottage.

GREEN TURTLE CLUB
Telephone: (809) 367-2572
The hub of dive and sailing activity on Green Turtle Cay, this sprawling club has 24 rooms scattered around garden-like grounds. The knotty-pine dining room and richly decorated bar, festooned with hundreds of sailing flags, are focal points of social activity among tourists. Lunch—including conch burgers and fritters—is served on an attractive patio overlooking the marina. Rates start at $82 double.

BLUFF HOUSE
Telephone: (809) 367-2786
Bluff House commands the best hotel vista on Green Turtle Cay. Situated on the cay's highest point, a 100-foot knoll, the main house and dining room look out across the sound for a beautiful view of New Plymouth. Its cottages and condominium-style accommodations are arranged on the slope down towards a fine beach. Rates are $75 double, $85 for suites.

RESTAURANTS
At the *SEA VIEW*, in "downtown" New Plymouth, Betty and Alphonso offer native Bahamian dishes and homemade pies. Dinner reservations required.

PLYMOUTH ROCK, near the main dock in New Plymouth, also serves Bahamian specialties and is open for breakfast, lunch and dinner.

LAURA'S SNACK BAR is a homey little hideaway on a back street behind the New Plymouth Inn. Formerly a cook at the Inn, Laura now prepares homecooked specialties, including chicken and fish, peas 'n rice, cole slaw, macaroni salads, several kinds of pie and homemade ice cream.

ROOSTER'S REST PUB AND RESTAURANT offers lunches of conch, chicken, burgers, and various sandwiches.

NOTES FROM MY JOURNAL
A traveling pentecostal crusade has set up its striped tent on the vacant corner lot across from the Inn in New Plymouth. Only two dozen worshipers attend the Saturday night revival. More curious onlookers are standing around in the street. The village's established churches are holding their own services tonight as well, the sermons and vocal choirs wafting from open windows in the warm night air. Walking down the dimly lit streets, we arrive at Miss Emily's Blue Bee Bar. Here's the action. We order our Goombay Smashes and continue walking under the moonlight. Over the hill, at Rooster's Rest, the crowd is feverish, dancing to the Gully Roosters. We watch, dance, then step outside for air and watch the stars. We walk again, out along the still harbor, and through the tranquil back streets of New Plymouth. Homemade ice cream at Laura's. It's wondrous that places like this even exist. The air is like velvet, the night is magical, the sense of peace carries us away.

HOW TO GET THERE
Bahamasair has regular flights into Treasure Cay by way of Marsh Harbor on Great Abaco. A taxi will take you to the landing, and a Green Turtle Ferry will carry you to your particular destination on Green Turtle Cay.

LONG ISLAND

After you land at the Deadman's Cay airstrip on Long Island and pick up your luggage, you might find yourself all alone outside the matchbox airport, which is closed and locked up in a matter of minutes after the flight arrives. You quickly begin to sense the real barrenness and desolation connoted by the airfield's name. If you have not already made arrangements for ground transportation, a few taxis will usually be on hand outside. Before he leaves, the airport manager can also make the necessary phone calls for you. Most travelers come to visit the Stella Maris Inn at the northern end of Long Island. But if you land at Deadman's Cay, be prepared for a rugged two-hour ride over a road where the potholes rival the pavement for total space.

Long Island, located 150 miles south of Nassau, was called Yuma by the Arawak Indians, Fernandina by Columbus after he visited it in 1492. Life could not have been all that much quieter on these 400 square miles five centuries ago. Stretching 90 miles north to south, the island has supported sheep farming, salt extraction operations, fishing, agriculture (pineapples, bananas, papayas and corn) and boat-building during its history. The largest segment of the 3300 population lives near the middle of the island, in and around Deadman's Cay which is adjoined by such settlements as Lower Deadman's Cay, MacKenzie, Buckley's, Cartwright and Mangrove Bush. The notorious Government Road runs north through Salt Pond, locale of the annual Long Island Regatta; Simms, an 18th-century seaport; to Stella Maris and Cape Santa Maria. To the south, the road leads to Clarence

Town, the island's capital; the Public and Chancery Ponds, Hard Bargain and South End. The adventurous explorer, who can withstand miles of poor road, will be able to investigate dozens of old Anglican and Catholic churches, such as St. Joseph's near Salt Pond, and St. Paul's and St. Peter's in Clarence Town. There are plantation ruins and attractive beaches in the southernmost reaches.

The western shores of Long Island, facing Exuma Sound, have the shallowest and gentlest waters, not unlike many coastlines in the Bahamas. But toward the northeast, the terrain is hilly and the coastline is surprisingly rugged and rocky. The waters here are especially good for scuba diving, with over 20 different spots identified for separate dives. With guidance from the dive masters at Stella Maris, you can even take a controlled dive to swim with the sharks at Shark Reef! Exploring colonial settlements that have changed slowly over time, enjoying the varied water sports and activities at Cape Santa Maria, and just getting away from nearly every sign of civilization are the reasons for a visit to this completely different sort of Long Island.

WHERE TO STAY
STELLA MARIS INN & ESTATE
Box 105
Long Island, Bahamas
Telephone: (809) 336-2106
Dominating the hills at the northern end of Long Island, this luxury resort sprawls out across acres and acres of scenic landscape dotted with coconut palms. Perhaps the effort required to get to Long Island deserves to be rewarded with a stay at this supremely attractive inn. Managed by two solicitous Germans, Peter Kuska and Jurg Friese, Stella Maris can accommodate 140 guests in a variety of rooms, cottages, townhouses, villas and deluxe bungalows. There are three swimming pools on the vast grounds and six beaches within walking

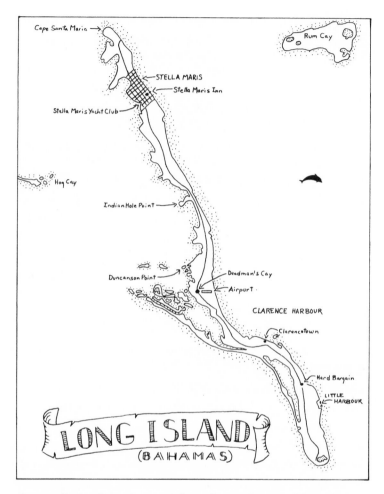

distance. Scuba diving is a specialty and water skiing and boat charters are available. The inn has its own airstrip, tennis courts, dining room and coffee shop, plus a reciprocal arrangement with the Cape Saint Maria Beach Club nine miles away on the sugarwhite sand of the Cape Santa Maria lagoon. Rates start at $60 single, $70 double in the summer ($68 single and $80 double in the winter) for simple rooms, and go up from there. Modified American Plan is available, as are package arrangements that include airfare, and/or scuba diving and fishing.

J.B. CARROLL'S GUEST HOUSE
Deadman's Cay, Long Island, Bahamas
Telephone: can be reached locally through Long Island operator.
For $40 a night, J.B. Carroll will put you up in one of the four bedrooms of his informal guest house, next to his market located on Government Road. He will pick you up at the airport if you call when you land, and will rent you one of his cars or jeeps so you can explore the island. In the morning he serves coffee in the dining room of his own house in the back. The Carroll guest rooms are homey but very small and simple. They share one bathroom, and the shower is not always functional. Around 11 p.m., J.B. turns off his generator, so out go your lights and off goes the fan.

RESTAURANTS
CONCHY'S: Carole Archer cried for three months when her husband, Lamond (or "Lammy") told her he was retiring from Xerox and they were moving from Nassau to Long Island. But in less than six months she decided she loved the remote island life. Now she helps Lammy run this small, cozy restaurant just a mile or so south of Stella Maris. Lammy has committed himself to learning his native Bahamian cuisine and has mastered a variety of dishes. Proudly, he showed us his kitchen and let us sample the steamed turtle and the minced lobster. His touch is well worth the $8 to $12 for dinner.

THOMPSON BAY INN: At Salt Pond, on the road between Deadman's Cay and Stella Maris, this modest restaurant bar serves ex-

cellent local seafood. If you call ahead, dinner will be ready when you arrive. We dropped in on our drive from Deadman's Cay to Stella Maris and returned to find a fresh, hearty meal waiting for us at the appointed time. The grouper and snapper are fried with native spices and served with spicy cole slaw, potato salad, and peas 'n rice. At about $6, dinner is a rare Bahamian bargain. Breakfasts are around $4, and fish or conch and chips snacks run about $3.50.

HOW TO GET THERE

Bahamasair flies from Nassau, sometimes by way of George Town, Exuma, to Deadman's Cay.

THE EXUMAS

During the drive from the tiny airport to the main settlement of George Town, Great Exuma, you begin to realize that having reached the Exumas, only 40 miles south east of Nassau, you are downshifting into the tranquil pace that continues to slow as you move south in the Bahamas. A taxi driver removes you from the momentary commotion that surrounds arrivals and departures at the airstrip, and carries you the few miles to George Town, a one-road town that is a fascinating mix of grand public and rustic private buildings. Although the majority of accommodations is located here, the town has a pervasive sleepy feeling that is extremely conducive to worry free relaxation and meditative strolls. Except in regatta and fishing contest seasons, this is as quickly as the pulse races in life in the Exumas.

The Exumas are comprised of some 90 miles of cays, with a population of 3700. Most people live on Great and Little Exuma, with 800 "concentrated" in George Town. The islands' colonial history took its most significant turn in the late 1700s, when Denys Rolle, took possession of 7000 acres on Great Exuma, establishing five cotton plantations worked by his transplanted population of slaves. Cotton never really succeeded as a cash crop on Exuma, and Rolle's son, Lord John Rolle presided over a failing empire until the emancipation of slaves in 1834. The Rolle land and name were subsequently passed down through the descendants of Rolle's slaves. Today, it is still the most prominent family name on Great Exuma. Jeremiah Rolle introduced tractor farming to the Exumas in mid-20th century, cultivating crops of giant sweet potatoes. When you land at the George Town airport, one of the first things you see is the sign reading "Kermit's," marking the bar/restaurant of Kermit Rolle, one of the island's leading entrepreneurs who also owns the Hilltop Tavern in (where else but?) Rolleville.

The architecture of George Town, like most of the settlements in the Exumas, harkens back to earlier centuries and proudly displays the islanders' penchant for pastel paints, especially pink and yellow. In the bend where the road curves around the point of beautiful Elizabeth Harbor, an enormous, broad-reaching tree spreads its limbs above a small but lovely Straw Market, where a few local women display and sell their handcrafted hats, baskets and other goods. Farther around the bend, past the impressive pink and white Government Administration Building and the Hotel Peace & Plenty, the 150-year-old St. Andrew's Anglican Church faces west, its brilliant white walls and royal blue doors and shutters almost glowing in the bright afternoon sun.

By rented car or public bus, you can explore outward, north and south, from George Town. To the south is Rolle Town, with its old, vibrantly painted buildings and a small bridge that links Great Exuma to Little Exuma. The small town of The Ferry affords wonderful views of the sea and is the home of 70-year-old Gloria Patience, "the Shark Lady," who catches sharks, sells their meat and makes jewelry from their teeth, for sale in her museum-like house. Just further south you can look out over Pretty Molly Bay from the Sand Dollar Beach Club before proceeding to Williams Town, site of the Old Hermitage or "Cotton House," a nearly 200-year-old plantation estate. To the north of George Town, you drive through Jimmy Hill, notable for great expanses of deserted beach; Mt. Thompson, near a large bay with the shadeless white-sand beach of Ocean Bight; and Steventon, before arriving at the charming hilltop village of Rolleville.

For snorkelers and divers, the Exumas offer a variety of underwater delights. The cays are surrounded by coral reefs at shallow and medium depths, and deeper wall diving reveals large formations of black coral. Blue holes, an uncharted Mystery Cave and various banks and cays invite exploration. The diving facilities include Wendle McGregor's personable Exuma Divers and the larger-scale Exuma Aquatics, affiliated with Hotel Pieces of Eight. After taking some guests out for a morning dive, Wendle McGregor took us in his boat to a superb snorkeling spot among the coral reefs that lie at the distant mouth of Elizabeth Harbour. The scuba sites are abundant and the explorers few. Only in March and April, during the Cruising (or Crazy) Regatta and the Out Island Regatta, when festive visitors swamp George Town, is Great Exuma's languorous peace transformed into hectic plenty.

FAVORITE SPOT
STOCKING ISLAND, about one mile offshore, protects Elizabeth Harbor from the Atlantic Ocean. Its miles of gorgeous, secluded beaches afford private sunbathing, excellent shelling and marvelous swimming. (Some speculate that this may have been Christopher Columbus' first landing in the New World, a conjecture that Salvadorans hotly dispute.) Its isolation and pristine beauty make it an ideal one-day escape into remote paradise. Boat transportation is available at Hotel Peace & Plenty for $5 (free to the hotel's guests).

WHERE TO STAY
PEACE & PLENTY
P.O. Box 55
George Town, Exuma, Bahamas
Telephone: (809) 336-2551
The oldest hotel in the Exumas, overlooking Elizabeth Harbor, was

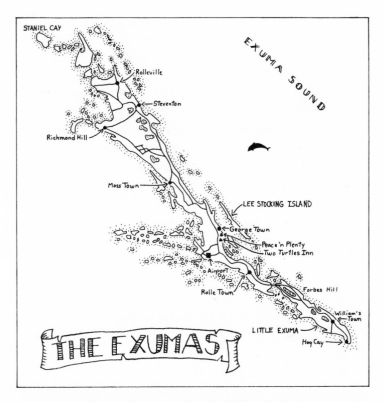

a sponge market until converted in the 1950s. Its distinctive pink-and-white painted buildings, with gabled roofs and dormer windows, add the charm needed to offset its size and tourist bustle. The popular hotel features 32 air-conditioned rooms (poolside, waterfront or garden suites), a swimming pool, an attractive indoor-outdoor dining room, two cocktail lounges, twice weekly dancing to live calypso, and courtesy boat transportation to Stocking Island. The lobby is a good place in which to glean information, from bulletin boards and staff, about what is happening in George Town. Rates are $68-74 for a double in the summer, and $94-98 during winter.

TWO TURTLES INN
P.O. Box 51
George Town, Exuma, Bahamas
Telephone: 1-800-336-2545

Located across the street from the Straw Market, near the bend in the road at Elizabeth Harbor, Two Turtles is a small, woodsy twelve-room motel-style inn. The trade-offs for the clean but ordinary accommodations are the relatively reasonable rates and lively, informal atmosphere. Locals and tourists gather at the cozy bar and in the pleasant courtyard for often boisterous discussions of news and events. The sunken cave-like dining room, carved out of rock, serves excellent local seafood and native dishes for breakfast, lunch and dinner, and the waitresses and cooks are very friendly. Some of the rooms are air-conditioned; all have ceiling fans and television. Rates are $48 summer, $60 winter, with four kitchenettes available at $55 and $70.

PIRATE'S POINT VILLAS
P.O. Box 23
George Town, Exuma, Bahamas
No telephone.

Three comfortable housekeeping villas, located on a private beach; each rents for $70 a day.

MARSHALL'S GUEST HOUSE
P.O. Box 27
George Town, Exuma, Bahamas
Telephone: (809) 336-2081

These very simple island accommodations—twelve rooms in a plain building off the beach in town—are fine for the budget traveler at $22 single and $30 double.

RESTAURANTS

All the Great Exuma hotels have good restaurants that serve different combinations of Bahamian, American and international cuisine in attractive dining areas. For very inexpensive home-cooked native meals, check out *LIZ & JIM'S*, a tiny, weathered shanty in George Town. *DARVILLE'S SUPPLIES* sells good home-made cakes and breads.

HOW TO GET THERE

Bahamasair has regularly scheduled service into George Town from Nassau. But be sure to re-check on all flights, as they are occasionally re-routed through Deadman's Cay depending on the number of potential passengers, or, as one woman put it, "With this flight you take your chances—they should have told you."

TURKS AND CAICOS

The Turks and Caicos have long been called the "forgotten islands." One hour and twenty minutes by jet southeast of Miami, this British crown colony consists of small islands with a total population of 9000 citizens scattered among eight inhabited islands. Even with increasing development as a tourist destination, there is still about one mile of private beach for each inhabitant! Part of the Bahama chain, the Turks and Caicos are flat islands with magnificent, empty beaches and the finest diving sites in the world.

The inhabited Caicos islands include Providenciales (with direct air service to Miami), North Caicos, Middle Caicos, East Caicos, Pine Cay and South Caicos. Across a 22-mile deep-water channel lie Grand Turk and Salt Cay in the Turks group.

PROVIDENCIALES ISLAND

Of all the Turks and Caicos islands, Providenciales (known locally as "Provo") offers the visitor the widest choice of hotel accommodations, restaurants and stores without spoiling its tranquil and friendly atmosphere. It is an island of peaceful rolling hills, a natural deep harbor, flowering cactus, and a spectacular coral reef for snorkeling, swimming and diving. At Northwest Point, a vertical dropoff to 6000 feet is considered by experts to be one of the finest diving sites in the world.

WHERE TO STAY

Although Barbara Francis, at the tourist bureau, said she could find "lodgin' with the locals," there are few bargains for the low-budget traveler on Provo. For the couple willing to pay at least $75 per night, there are several choices.

ISLAND PRINCESS HOTEL
Reservations: Box 52-6002
Miami, Florida 33152
Telephone: (809) 946-4260
Each room has its own veranda, ceiling fan and big sliding glass windows. The beach front location is ideal for families and the general

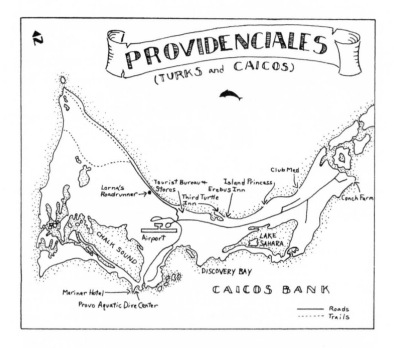

ambience is informal and friendly. The staff is extremely helpful and pleasant and the dining room provides excellent food: local dishes, fresh fish, homemade breads. Complete watersport facilities are offered: windsurfing, diving, bonefishing, snorkeling. The dive shop is a full service International Training Facility and for the serious diver, Provo offers untouched underwater walls, gardens, reefs and wrecks. $65 single, $75 double; special dive packages are available.

MARINER HOTEL
Sapodilla Point
Providenciales, Turks and Caicos
B.W.I.
Telephone: (809) 946-4488
Landscaped in a tropical setting, this immaculate 25-room hotel is

located on a secluded and peaceful knoll just a three minute walk to a fine beach, five minutes to the Provo Aquatic Center (diving, sail and motor boat rentals, windsurfer sailboards). Although I preferred the food at the Islander, the Mariner was my favorite room choice on Provo. Rates: $65 single, $75 for two.

EREBUS INN
Turtle Cove
Providenciales, Turks and Caicos
B.W.I.
Telephone: (809) 946-4240
On a hillside overlooking Turtle Cove, a short walk to the beach, shops and restaurants, the Erebus has six rooms facing the marina, four individual bungalows, each with a large balcony, and 22 spacious new rooms. Swimming pool, spa, air conditioning, telephones. Rooms start at $60 single, $70 for two; bungalows are $80 single, $90 for two.

RESTAURANTS
ISLAND PRINCESS HOTEL. Excellent buffet dinners with fresh island produce, grilled or baked fish.

HENRY'S ROADRUNNER, Blue Hills. A very casual local restaurant, famous for its Wednesday night buffets which feature lobster, conch, grouper, barbecued ribs, turtle and steaks, red beans and rice. Reasonable. Tel. 4216.

GILLEY'S CAFE. A bar-restaurant at the airport, excellent for lobster salad, lobster sandwiches and homemade chili.

NOTEWORTHY
Social life on Provo centers around the church: the choirs and the

Church of God Band should not be missed. Church services and singing last all day Sunday, and it is quite acceptable to attend a service and leave at any time.

SCUBA enthusiasts will head straight for Northwest Point for some of the finest diving in the world; but the less ambitious or experienced visitor can get a view of coral and other marine life from the glass-bottom "Grouper Snooper" which operates regular boat excursions.

CAICO CONCH FARM. At the far eastern end of Provo, the world's first conch mariculture facility welcomes visitors. The distinctive glass-covered geodesic dome and large silver water tanks are easily recognized from land or sea. Inside, the fascinating farming of this fast-disappearing staple food takes place, from hatched conch eggs in controlled sea egg farms, to large larval tanks where they are fed and nurtured to maturity. The gift shop at the farm specializes in unique conch jewelry and rare conch pearls.

WEATHER
Although in a tropical location, the climate of the Turks and Caicos is free from excessive humidity. Rainfall averages 30 inches per year, falling mainly in April, May, September, October and November. Temperatures average 77 degrees on winter days, and 83 degrees in the summer.

IMMIGRATION
Passports are not required of U.S. and Canadian citizens, but some form of identification, such as a birth certificate or voter's registration card, should be taken.

PINE CAY

Pine Cay is one of a chain of islets connecting Providenciales and North Caicos. Two miles long and covering 800 acres, it is a small, private residential community with one 12-room hotel run as a nature preserve.

For the traveler who does not have to ask the price, the small and comfortable Meridian Club provides the ultimate escape from the rigors of the 20th century. The two-mile beach is one of the finest in the Caribbean, and, of course, it is never crowded. There are a freshwater pool, tennis court, windsurfing, a nature trail featuring a wide variety of birds and plants, and outstanding snorkeling, diving and fishing.

Off season rates (April 1-July 31, and November 1-December 18) are $140 single, $200 for two, including three meals a day, free use of sailboats, bicycles and snorkeling gear, boating excursions to neighboring islands, and free postage stamps!

MERIDIAN CLUB
Pine Cay
Turks and Caicos, B.W.I.
Reservations: New York (212) 696-4566

NOTEWORTHY
FORT GEORGE CAY NATIONAL PARK. Off the north coast of Pine

Cay there are ruins of a British fort. With the help of a local guide, traces of pre-Columbian settlements can be found in this unique park.

WATER CAY AND LITTLE WATER CAY. Off the south coast, these tiny islands are a shell collector's dream.

NORTH CAICOS

Nature lovers will find an earthly paradise on North Caicos. This large and most northerly of the chain is also the most fertile. Limes, papayas, sapodillas, oranges, tamarinds and grapefruit abound. Endless beautiful beaches ring the island. Charming villages, quiet walks, and unusual species of birds are among its wonders.

NOTEWORTHY

FLAMINGO POND, to the south of Whitby, harbors a nesting place for exotic flamingos, now rare in the wild state.

BOTTLE CREEK SETTLEMENTS. Six miles southeast of Whitby, this quiet settlement has changed little since the 19th century. Inhabitants live mainly off fresh fish, crayfish and shellfish. Beautiful beaches offer long, solitary walks and swims in the crystal clear water.

FAVORITE SPOT

THREE MARY CAYS: Four miles west of Whitby by boat, Three Mary Cays is a haven of unspoiled beauty, fine beaches and clear water. There are Limestone caves to explore on the north coast, and my favorite secluded beach is nearby at Mudjin Harbor.

WHERE TO STAY
PELICAN BEACH HOTEL
North Caicos
Turks and Caicos, B.W.I.
Telephone: (809) 946-4692
North Caicos native Clifford Gardiner owns and operates this friendly eight-room hotel. Daily rate of $50 per person includes full breakfast and dinner. There are ten miles of uncrowded white sand beach at your doorstep. Equipment is available for day sailing, snorkeling and scuba.

PROSPECT OF WHITBY HOTEL
Whitby, North Caicos
Turks and Caicos, B.W.I.
Telephone: (809) 946-4250
Situated on a seven-mile long stretch of beach, Prospect of Whitby Hotel provides the amenities of a swimming pool, tennis, dive shop and water sports. The expense pays off in the lack of crowds and the minimal commercial development. New owners Richard Jaross and Saudi West hope to have a small garden soon for fresh produce.

MIDDLE CAICOS

With a population of only 1000 residents, Grand Caicos or Middle
Caicos as it is often called is the largest and least developed of any
of the inhabited Turks and Caicos. This attractive island, with magnificent beaches and beautiful scenery, is also the most interesting. For
the adventurous traveler interested in archeology and geology, Middle
Caicos is a veritable untrodden paradise. Along the northern coast,
towering limestone cliffs drop sharply to placid, white secluded
beaches. These bluffs offer a dramatic panorama seldom experienced
on other sub-tropical islands.

Conch Bar is the major of three settlements and the location of
the island's only telephone, guesthouse and airplane runway. Nearby
are the barely explored, cathedral-size caves where Lucayan Indian
artifacts have recently been discovered. The caves are impressive:
pure white stalactites and stalagmites and mysterious underground
salt lakes. Several of the entrances to the different caves are slightly
hidden by large calcite pillars, while some are under water. However,
once the entrances are located, there is no difficulty finding the various chambers.

Between the villages of Bambarra and Lorimer are the interesting
ruins of a settlement of the Arawak and Lucayan Indians. Two miles
south is Big Pond, a rich and varied plant and animal life nature
reserve.

At Douglas Taylor's four-room Guest House in Conch Bar settlement, visitors are greeted by some of the most hospitable inhabitants

of these islands. Douglas Taylor can arrange island excursions or bone-fishing, or point you in the right direction for excellent beachcombing and shelling among the secluded hideaways on the northern coast.

DOUGLAS TAYLOR'S GUEST HOUSE
Conch Bar Settlement
Middle Caicos
Turks and Caicos, B.W.I.
Telephone: (809) 946-3322

SOUTH CAICOS ISLAND

South Caicos Island has long been an important export-oriented fishing center. Along the west coast, the shallow water of the Caicos bank is the home of the most important single industry—the harvesting and export of conch and spiny lobster.

But South Caicos is far from spoiled by its industry. The southern coast offers outstanding diving and beautiful beaches of white sand. There is easy access to fine diving along the drop-off with wall diving only minutes from shore. The scuba diver will delight in the multitude and variety of marine life. Large pelagic fish populate this area, as well as loggerhead turtles, barracudas, spotted eagle rays, octopus, grouper and snapper.

Cockburn Harbour, the main settlement, is the best natural harbor in the Caicos Islands and provides good protection for yachts in almost any weather. Here you will find grocery stores, a clinic, a telephone station, and overnight accommodations. A good view of Cockburn Harbour can be enjoyed from Highlands, a 19th century house.

WHERE TO STAY
ADMIRAL INN
Cockburn Harbor
South Caicos
Turks and Caicos, B.W.I.
Telephone: (809) 946-3223
Rates: $40 for two

SALT CAY ISLAND

Just five minutes by air from Grand Turk, Salt Cay is a peaceful, quiet and colorful island with a magnificent beach bordering the north coast. The windmills that once powered the salt industry add an exotic touch to the landscape, and 19th century architecture slowly turns to ruins in the warm Salt Cay sun.

WHERE TO STAY

There is only one telephone on Salt Cay, but you can leave a message for any of the island's three lodgings. (809) 946-2485.

AMERICAN HOUSE
Salt Cay
Turks and Caicos, B.W.I.
The American House was constructed in 1839 and has recently been refurbished. Rooms are large and airy, many with verandas built in the Bermuda style. The ocean is only 25 feet from the back door! Rates: $50 per room.

MOUNT PLEASANT GUEST HOUSE
Salt Cay
Turks and Caicos, B.W.I.
Simple accommodations and renowned native dishes are featured at this five-room guest house, a friendly home-away-from-home. Rates:

$95 daily for two, all meals included.

THE WINDMILLS AT SALT CAY
U.S. Reservations Office:
Salt Cay Company
416 Goldsboro Street
Easton, MD 21601
Telephone: (301) 822-6306
The Windmills offers comfortable and expensive accommodations for those who want no telephones, no radios, no television or newspapers. Owners Patricia and Guy Lovelace have created a tasteful retreat where one may rent a room, cottage or a suite with private pool on a lonely two-mile stretch of beach.

GRAND TURK ISLAND

Divers are often the first visitors to discover an unspoiled island. That certainly is the case with Grand Turk, a six-mile long British colony with a flat, sandy coastline and 19th century capitol at Cockburn Town. Flying in on an eight-passenger TAC National plane, I could see the dive boats parked along the island's reef.

While the divers had obviously come for the island's offshore attractions, this is also an island to enjoy by foot or bike. The buildings facing the sea along Front Street are in a charming weathered state, reflecting their age and endurance. On a narrow side street, horses graze on the dry lawn of an abandoned house. This sleepy, endearing town has just enough amenities for comfort without spoiling its 19th century colonial past. Minuscule restaurants, some with just one table, occupy the boat houses along the sea.

The salt mines started by settlers from Bermuda once brought wealth and prosperity to Grand Turk, inspiring the construction of a number of fine buildings and churches: Waterloo House (1815), now the Governor's residence; a Victorian library; an attractive wood and limestone Government House, which is still the colony's administrative center.

Facing the beach near town, the 180-year-old main house of Salt Raker Inn looked inviting. Once I saw the rear garden and attractive open-air dining area, I knew I would be settling in for awhile.

The gracious hospitality of the new owners more than compensated for the inn's slight look of disrepair. They were fresh from Eng-

land with enthusiastic plans to overcome the inn's deferred maintenance. Martin unlocked one of the garden sheds and presented me
with a bicycle. I was off in a flash to explore this quiet, friendly island.

FAVORITE SPOT
SWIMMING: GOVERNOR'S BEACH, only a ten-minute bicycle
ride from town, offers excellent swimming and snorkeling.

SCUBA: The diving on Grand Turk is superb. The 6000-foot deep
underwater "Grand Canyon" of coral is one of the natural wonders
of the world. The diving instructors at Turks Island Divers Ltd. are
excellent and will point out incredible marine creatures, purple tube
sponges, and black coral.

TURKS ISLANDS DIVERS LTD.
Kittina Hotel, Box 42
Grand Turk
Turks and Caicos, B.W.I.
Telephone: (809) 946-2386

RESTAURANTS
Directly on the beach at the north of Front Street, Peanuts Snak Shop
has but one table and a few benches. Friendly owner, Peanuts But-
terfield cooks delicious conch fritters on her little outdoor gas burner.
Ask to see her family photo album.

TURKS HEAD. A thatched roof shelters diners at this century-old
establishment which serves consistently good food, especially the
fish dishes.

WHERE TO STAY
COLUMBUS HOUSE
Box 97
Grand Turk
Turks and Caicos, B.W.I.
Telephone: (809) 946-2517

The Columbus, named after the discoverer of the New World (whose landfall is believed by some to have taken place at Grand Turk, and not at San Salvador as commonly held), is a quaint, two-story roadside inn, 150 feet from the main beach. Rates: $35 single, $50 double, with discounts for longer term guests. Dive packages also available.

TURKS HEAD INN
P.O. Box 58
Grand Turk
Turks and Caicos, B.W.I.
Telephone: (809) 946-2466

Located in an old garden with towering trees, this romantic 100-year-old inn has a split-level covered veranda, and four-poster beds. Adjacent to the inn are the Driftwood Cottages, which rent for $75 per night. Rooms in the main lodge, facing the sea, range from $45 for a single to $70 for a double.

SALT RAKER INN
Box 1
Grand Turk
Turks and Caicos, B.W.I.
Telephone: (809) 946-2260

The informal 180-year-old main house is of Bermudian architecture and includes three large, airy suites overlooking the sea at Salt Raker's own beach. In the lodge you will find a well-stocked library, maps, and travel information. In the back, several basic cottages are scattered throughout the garden. The manager-owner is very warm and helpful. Rates start at $50 single, $65 double.

HOTEL KITTINA
Grand Turk
Turks and Caicos, B.W.I.
Telephone: (809) 946-2232
Just a few feet from the beach, the Kittina has 43 clean, modern rooms and is the largest hotel on the island. Rooms in the two-story structure face the sea or a courtyard. Rates range from $75 for two, to $125 for an oceanfront suite.

WEATHER
The climate is sub-tropical and weather conditions are mild, with plenty of sunshine and low humidity year round. Summer temperatures average 88F with highs recorded at 100 degrees F in the Salt Islands.

Winter temperatures are a little cooler, averaging 77F, with the average daytime temperature in the mid 80s. Constant easterly trade winds lessen the effect of humidity and provide pleasant cool breezes in the evening.

"There is no rainy season. May and November are the wettest months, with the most rainfall occurring in the western islands and cays." (From *The Pilot's Guide*)

NOTEWORTHY
BIRDWATCHING: Gibb and Round Cay Bird Sanctuaries are home to many interesting species.

MUSIC: Ask around town for ripsaw music. You may be lucky and

ATLANTIC OCEAN

NORTH CREEK

Peanut's Snack Shop

Library/P.O. Office

Turk's Head Inn

Salt Raker Inn

GRAND TURK (Cockburn Town)

The Island Cemetery

Town Pond

Governor's Residence

Island's Best Beach (In front of Governor's Residence)

Airport

Gun Hill Fort

Columbus Landfall 1492

GRAND TURK

get a chance to hear Joe Robinson and his Grand Turk High School Dancers, led by Terry Robinson. Music on Grand Turk is informal and non-commercial.

CAMPING: No public camping facilities are provided in the islands; however, camping is permitted. It is recommended that you contact local police or island magistrate, stating your intentions and the proposed location of your campsite.

GOOD BUYS: For under a dollar one can buy a handful of fascinating Turks and Caicos stamps. My purchase of a series of 18th century boats will make a fine gift, either framed or laminated as a book mark. The Post Office is easy to find on Front Street, next to the government offices.

It seemed fitting that I would leave this friendly island with the only plates of the next issue of the *CONCH NEWS*. The paper's new owner-editor had entrusted me, a virtual total stranger, with their safe delivery to the printer in Miami. The airport waiting room could hardly be called crowded: there were only six of us flying out that day to Providenciales and Miami. My fellow passengers, the governor, his wife and male secretary-bodyguard, fit their British role as perfectly as E.M. Forster characters. As they sat beside me on the eight-passenger plane, I thought, what a pleasant and relaxed assignment they must have: not too much work, a fine colonial house to call home, and the island's best beach only steps away.

PUERTO RICO

Over the past decade, a few selective travelers have discovered the secluded delights of two relatively unknown Puerto Rican islands, Vieques and Culebra. Visited by Columbus on his second New World voyage in 1493, and once known as the Spanish Virgin Islands, these two small islands are only a few miles off the east coast of Puerto Rico, but they remain essentially undiscovered by tourists. Throughout most of the 20th century, they have been under the jurisdiction of the United States. From 1901, Culebra was the site of a naval reservation, and from World War II through the mid-1970s, the island was used for U.S. Navy gunnery and bombing practice. There is no longer a military presence on Culebra. In 1948, the Navy took possession of two-thirds of the land on Vieques, and while both the Navy and Marines maintain training bases on the island, much of the land has been leased for cattle grazing. The sailors and Marines seem to have a minimal impact on life on Vieques, although their presence is still an object of native protest. The populations of both Culebra and Vieques have grown in the past decade, after a precipitous decline caused by military maneuvers. Now the two islands are characterized by an easygoing social atmosphere to complement the splendid weather, beautiful geography and relaxing pace.

VIEQUES

On the drive from the tiny airport on the north coast of Vieques, through the four miles of rolling hills to Esperanza, on the south side of the island where most vacationers stay, the unique appeal of this Puerto Rican island begins to reveal itself. Cattle graze contentedly on the scrubby hillsides, accompanied by the lanky, white Africa egrets that keep them free of insects. Arching expanses of white beach flash into view through lush foliage. Sunlight filters through palm, mango and flamboyant trees, dappling the roadway with dazzling patterns of shadow and light. A mere six miles from the east end of Puerto Rico, Vieques is light years removed from the frantic pace of modern civilization. This 51-square-mile island (21 miles long and one to five miles wide) boasts some of the most beautiful beaches in the Caribbean and a way of life that harkens back to another century.

Once the home of 25,000 Spanish-speaking people, Vieques was a major sugar producing island. None of the four sugar mills remains today, however, and the population is down to about 8000, most of whom depend on cattle farming, fishing and light industry for their livelihood, and live in the central section of island, between the eastern and western U.S. military reserves. The chief town is Isabel Segunda on the northern side, with about 3500 residents. But most visitors stay near Esperanza, a strip of beach on the southern coast. Vieques was used as a location for the films *Lord of the Flies* and *Heartbreak Ridge*, but the island is noted far more for its magnificent beaches and abundant wildlife which includes birds, lizards, crabs, mongeese, and wild *paso fino* (fine-gait) horses. The temperature seldom varies much from 80 degrees year round, with refreshing breezes blowing in from the sea, and rainfall averaging only 47 inches per year. Diving, snorkeling and nighttime trips to the spectacular Phosphorescent Bay are available through Vieques Divers in Esperanza.

Getting around the island is remarkably easy, whether or not you rent a jeep, car, motor scooter or bicycle. The public vans, publicos, will pick you up and drop you off anywhere on their route for one dollar, and for a negotiated fee they will become taxis, taking you wherever you like. Once you are in Esperanza or Isabel Segunda, everything is within walking distance.

One of our favorite walks was from Sun Bay, near Esperanza, to Media Luna and Navia. For much of the morning, we were the only swimmers on the vast expanse of beach at Sun Bay. Walking along the road that winds around to Media Luna, we encountered mongeese and several of the island's small wild horses. Although there were signs of previous visitors to this sheltered bay, once again we were

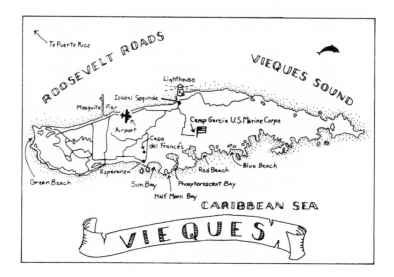

alone on the beach. Continuing on to Navia, we finally encountered a "crowd," about six other people on the long strip of white sand. We spent the rest of the afternoon watching the sand crabs dart in and out of their holes, and napping in the softening afternoon sunshine, lulled by the sounds of the breeze and the surf.

The island of Vieques is not all that remote—being so easily accessible from Puerto Rico—but with its many secluded beaches, scattered population and light tourist trade, it has all the advantages of being off the beaten track.

FAVORITE SPOTS

You could spend weeks just exploring the many beaches of Vieques, and all are worth investigating.

SUN BAY is a mile-and-a-half long, crescent-shaped beach in a public park just east of Esperanza. Coconut palms lines the shore, providing ample shade. The one- to two-foot waves are just high enough to make swimming interesting. The government maintains the beach, parking lot, picnic tables and bathhouse, but a "crowd" might amount to a dozen people on the entire beach. Admission is $1 per car.

MEDIA LUNA ("Half Moon") is a small, enclosed beach further to the east from Sun Bay. Here you can wade out a hundred yards or more in warm, absolutely still water.

NAVIA (also called "Third Beach") is beyond Media Luna, and is one of the most beautiful on the island. Waves roll in from the ocean past a rocky promontory, and sand crabs dash in and out of their holes in the beach.

GREEN BEACH, at the western end of Vieques, is accessible, with a day pass, through the naval reservation. It is long, empty and gorgeous, affording a fine view back to Puerto Rico.

ISABEL SEGUNDA, the main population center of Vieques, was founded in 1843 and is worth a morning or afternoon of exploration. A deserted lighthouse, built in 1896, rises 68 feet above the harbor. High on the hill behind town, El Fortin, a partially restored 145-year-old Spanish fort, the last one constructed in New World, allows a grand view of the city and the northern coastline.

WHERE TO STAY

CASA DEL FRANCES
P.O. Box 458
Vieques, Puerto Rico 00765
Telephone: (809) 741-3751
Irving Greenblatt, a cantankerous retired businessman from Boston, runs what many people consider to be "the only place to stay" on Vieques. His hotel is a revamped turn-of-the-century French sugar plantation, sitting on a hill above Esperanza. The downstairs rooms have 17-foot ceilings and open out onto sunny verandas. Not all rooms are equally spacious or ideally located. Meals are served in a classically "tropical," partially-open dining room overlooking the cloistered swimming pool, and evening socializing revolves around a charming outdoor bar, surrounded by the lush garden foliage. Irving is one of the island's most notable characters, and his staff takes good care of the Casa guests, many of whom return year after year. But the marvelous old building itself is showing distressing signs of disrepair and will soon need the kind of serious attention that Irving puts into creating atmosphere.

Rates in the summer season, April 30 to December 1, are $55; in the winter, December 1 to April 30, $69. Note: $15 per person is

automatically added for continental breakfast and dinner. Also added are a 6% room tax and a 15% service charge in lieu of gratuities.

POSADA VISTA MAR
P.O. Box 495
Vieques, Puerto Rico 00765
Telephone: (809) 741-8716 or 8719

The best bargain, the most gracious hospitality and the best native cooking are available at this humble guesthouse on a low hill beyond the west end of Esperanza. An unbelievably thoughtful native Vieques woman named Olga rents out a half dozen small, clean but spartan rooms behind her screened-in restaurant. The sounds of crickets and the island's famous tree frogs (*coqi*) create a vibrant chorus at night, and the bleating of Olga's goats combines with the crowing of roosters in the early morn. When it was time for us to catch a ferry to Fajardo, Olga woke us up before dawn, served us "coffee on the house," and said goodbye with a kiss. Rates are $20 per night, including tax. Olga also has an apartment available for longer rentals.

THE TRADE WINDS
C. Mellado 360
Vieques, Puerto Rico 00765
Telephone: (809) 741-8666 or 8368

Located on the strip at Esperanza, this well maintained guesthouse provides fairly modern accommodations right across the road from the beach. Rates are $35.50 single and $45.50 double, with two-bedroom houses renting for $60 and $65 per night.

VILLA ESPERANZA
Calle Flamboyan, Esperanza
Vieques, Puerto Rico 00765
Telephone: (809) 741-8588

This ambitious parador, situated on the site of an old sugar plantation at the east end of Esperanza, has modern villa apartments, in configurations that can be rented as one- or two-bedroom units. The closest thing to a resort on Vieques, Villa Esperanza features a restaurant, tennis courts, scooter and jeep rentals, and private beach access. Rates are $90 double.

RESTAURANTS

POSADA VISTA MAR offers superb and inexpensive native cuisine, specializing in fried whole fish—grouper or snapper—served with rice and *arepas*.

EL QUENEPO, across the street from the beach at Esperanza, is operated by the garrulous Mario, a former Brooklyn resident, who returned to Vieques and now prepares all varieties of seafood (crab, fish, lobster, octopus, conch) specializing in soups and salads as well as entrees. For lunch, a meal of black beans, rice and *arepas* is perfect.

BANANAS is the "hot spot" at Esperanza, attracting what young tourist crowd there is to its outdoor bar facing the beach. It is especially popular with those who want a taste of such American standards as burgers, chili and pizza, and offers the most active night life on the weekends. Bananas also has several very basic rooms for rent in the back.

THE TRADE WINDS boasts the best ocean view from its attractive restaurant and bar to go along with its popular lunch and dinner menus of creative meat and seafood dishes.

HOW TO GET THERE

Crownair flies ten-seat planes to Vieques from San Juan's Isla Verde

International Airport, and other airlines such as Air Link and Flamenco, fly in from Isla Grande Airport. A 400 passenger ferry leaves Fajardo, on the east end of Puerto Rico, twice daily and arrives at the terminal in Isabel Segunda. Publico service is available from both the Vieques airport and Isabel Segunda to your destination on Vieques.

CULEBRA

At El Mini-Mas market in central Dewey, Winnie and Virginia stand behind the counter and generously share stories and information about their island. They warn that in February and March the hotels and guesthouses are "booked solid" (with about 100 vacationers). They recommend returning in April to watch thousands of sooty terns build their nests on the island's rocky ledges. They explain that the strange garden down the street—the one full of ceramic animals, painted truck tires, sea shells and tortoise shells arranged into novel sculptures—belongs to "Cato," Winnie's aunt. They express their pleasure at the fact that few tourists come over from Puerto Rico, thus leaving their island to bask in its tranquil isolation. The unforced friendliness of Winnie and Virginia, and the undisturbed natural wonders of Culebra which they describe, are at the heart of this charming, unspoiled island's appeal.

On Puerto Rico and even on nearby Vieques, most people tell you that there is "nothing to do" on Culebra. They could not be further off the mark. A National Wildlife Refuge, mangrove forests, spectacular beaches, a sheltered deep-water bay, and extensive coral reefs are among the scenic attractions complemented by the warm hospitality of the nearly 2000, mostly English-speaking residents. The 11-square-mile island, located 19 miles east of Puerto Rico, is the largest of 24 islands and cays that make up a small-scale archipelago. Culebra is teeming with wildlife, including sea turtles, giant lizards, and more than 85 species of birds. Its rolling hills, rising to gentle 300-foot peaks, invite exploration on foot or bicycle.

The human population, mostly descended from Spanish settlers, is centered in the small sleepy town of Dewey (known locally as "Puebla"), located on beautiful Ensenada Honda ("deep bay"). About 300 Culebrans work at the pharmaceutical equipment manufacturing company in Dewey, and most others, including several dozen transplanted North Americans and Europeans, are self-employed in services or fishing. Full employment and social harmony keep the island crime-free and wonderfully relaxed. Although the architecture of Dewey is unremarkable, barely reflecting the island's Spanish origins, the town is nonetheless attractive, with an impressive government building, interesting churches, a charming post office, an irresistible bakery, and pastel-colored houses packed close together on narrow streets. Culebra would seem ripe for development, and the number

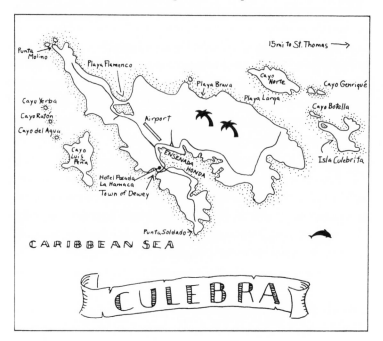

of cars and trucks on the roads is indeed surprising. But the island's reliance on rainwater, gathered in rooftop cisterns, and the preservation of lands in the National Refuge restrict the rate and scope of growth. Private homes for vacationers and retirees continue to be built outside Dewey, but large-scale tourist development seems unlikely. One of the small pleasures on Culebra is to look up and see the airplanes carrying tourists from San Juan to St. Thomas, only 14 miles away, and know that most of the passengers will not even notice the undiscovered island below.

FAVORITE SPOTS

PLAYA FLAMENCO, on the north coast, is the most spectacular of Culebra's many fine beaches. The surf can be rough, but it does not inhibit swimming, and you are likely to find yourself the sole visitor on nearly a mile of clean, white sand.

CULEBRITA, (like Cayo Luis Pena), is a large cay that is part of the Wildlife Refuge and is home to the endangered hawksbill turtle. The nearby mile-long coral formation is one of the finest diving and snorkeling spots in the region. Culebra's offshore cays can be reached by hiring a local fishing or sailboat.

MOUNT RESACA is a large unit of the Refuge land on the northern side of Culebra. It is marked by large sections of dry subtropical forest, with fascinating vegetation including thorn thickets, palms and cactus. The huge boulder formations support beautiful varieties of orchids, bromeliads and peperomia.

NOTEWORTHY

JOHANNA'S FANTASY ISLAND, tucked away in a remote mangrove swamp, is the dream hideaway of Johanna Taylor, who built her own home in the exotic tangle of mangrove roots. A hired boat can carry you up to her dock, and if she is home, Johanna comes out and offers 25-cent tours and shows the jewelry and souvenirs that she crafts by hand.

WHERE TO STAY
POSADA LA HAMACA
Box 186
Culebra, Puerto Rico 00645
Telephone: (809) 742-3516
In late 1986, Chuck and Marlene Selby took over Posada La Hamaca, managing the small two-story hotel for an investment group from the Virgin Islands. The neat but somewhat stark accommodations include six hotel rooms upstairs and three efficiency units downstairs. Located in Dewey on the canal leading to Ensenada Honda, the hotel features an "honor bar" and barbecue on the canal-side patio, and a covered rooftop lounge (under construction in 1987) overlooking the bay. Chuck provides van transportation to Flamenco Beach. Rates start at $30 double (plus a 6% hotel tax).

CLUB SEABOURNE
Fulladosa Road, Ensenada Honda
Telephone: (809) 742-3839
About a mile or so outside Dewey, the Seabourne is situated on a hillside with a fine view of Ensenada Honda. A spectacular flower garden slopes up to the swimming pool, screened outdoor dining room and patio bar. The Seaborne offers rooms with full kitchen facilities starting at $75 per night, double.

CORAL ISLAND GUEST HOUSE
Waterfront, Dewey
Telephone: (809) 742-3177, (617) 545-5120

Located across the street from the ferry terminal, this simple hotel offers rooms for $30 per day, and complete apartments, with kitchens, for $100. Some rooms have balconies overlooking the harbor and the town, but this is a very basic spot, probably best for people who will spend most of their time enjoying such water sports as windsurfing and diving.

WEEKLY RENTALS

A wide variety of fully furnished apartments, cottages and houses is available for short- and long-term rentals. Full information can be provided by the Tourism Office, Box 56, Culebra, Puerto Rico 00645. Telephone (809) 742-3521 or 742-3116.

CIELO Y MAR GUEST HOUSE *and* PUNTA ALOE VILLAS
Box 207
Culebra, Puerto Rico 00645
Telephone: (809) 742-3167
or
Pan Yatrakis
305 Judd Road
Easton, CT 06612
Telephone: (203) 268-4964 or 261-7344

Located out of town at Punta Aloe, overlooking Ensenada Honda, these are modern, fully equipped houses and apartments, with a vast array of amenities, appliances and conveniences. They start at $295 per week for one or two people and go up to $650 per week for three to six people.

RESTAURANTS

EL PESCADOR, in downtown Dewey, serves delicious island food, including shark *empanadas*, pimiento rellenos, lobster soup, *pastilillos*, *arepa*, and flan, as well as steaks, chops and pasta dishes. Louisa, the Brooklyn-born waitress, has lived in Culebra for 15 years and can share stories in her free moments.

MARTA'S ISLAND DELI, in downtown Dewey close to the ferry landing, offers a variety of local seafood, served either indoors, near the bar, or in an enclosed garden patio.

EL BATAY, located on the road leading out of town towards the airport, is a stark bar/pool room that serves delicious, inexpensive grilled sandwiches on locally baked bread.

CLUB SEABOURNE boasts the most elegant, and most expensive (in the $15 to $20 range) dining on Culebra, with seafood and continental dishes prepared by a French cook and served in an attractive dining area overlooking beautiful Ensenada Honda.

HOW TO GET THERE

From the Puerto Rico mainland, daily ferry service is provided from Fajardo (on the eastern end of the island, a long drive from San Juan). The fare for the two-hour trip is about $2.50.

Flamenco Airways flies out of the Isla Grande Airport in San Juan (20 minutes from the International Airport). The 30 minute flight costs about $23. There is also less frequent air service from St. Thomas and Vieques.

LEEWARD ISLANDS

SABA

If all you ever did on Saba was fly in and land, and then take off again, you would have experienced one of the most exhilarating adventures in the Caribbean. Imagine an airstrip that looks like a small stretch of sidewalk. Place it at the tip of a green volcanic island that rises suddenly and dramatically out of the deep blue sea. At either end of the runway, rocky cliffs drop off precipitously to the water 130 feet below. And at one end, the edge of the strip abuts the mountainside. "Of course, we're going to approach from the end that juts out over the water," you think, as your tiny, twin-engine, ten-seat STOL (Short Take-Off and Landing) airplane circles out over the ocean. Then your pilot swings the plane around, and your heart jumps into your throat. The plane is aimed directly at the side of the mountain! Your breath stops short and your knuckles turn white. The plane makes a quick bank to the left. . .and before you know it, there's the runway. "We can't land at that angle!" the voice in your head cries. But before you can gasp again, the plane has touched down and stopped, using less than half of the 1300-foot airstrip.

After landing on one of the shortest runways in the world, you might think that little else on this tiny chunk of Netherlands Antilles could measure up for excitement. But remarkably, what lies in store on this five-square mile Dutch island is all uphill. When you clear customs in the picturesque cottage-like airport, Saban taxivans are waiting to take you from Flat Point (indeed, virtually the only flat point on Saba) up the steep road through 19 serpentine curves, through Hell's Gate, to your destination in the equally accurately named Windwardside or over the mountain to The Bottom. Your driver will probably tell you how the road was hand-built, without any machinery, over the course of 20 years, from 1940 to 1960; that prior to that time, all goods were carried from one side of the island to the other over a grueling series of steps; and that only recently have the stone walls and eroded sections of concrete begun to be rebuilt.

As the drive continues, you might have to pinch yourself to make sure that you are not dreaming up this fairy-tale island. The buildings, painted pristine white with glossy green trim and brick-red roofs, look as though they have been preserved and transplanted from some remote European Alpine village. The flowers hanging over the wall along the road create an eye-catching riot of color against the unbroken background of rich green foliage. And the views forward, up the mountain where misty clouds brush across the ridges, and back, down the steep slopes and canyons to the sea, leave you as breathless as did your landing.

Before you have reached either of Saba's two main villages, Windwardside or The Bottom, your driver will have shared a wealth of information. Helpful tips and personal stories flow freely from most of the 1000 black and white residents of Saba, one of the friendliest islands in the Caribbean. For instance, there is Carmen, who works as waitress and bartender at Scout's Place by night, drives her own taxivan during the day, and is building a new house on the hillside overlooking The Bottom. A native of Saba, she can relate a book full of family and local history. At the Around the Bend clothing shop in Windwardside, Frida Johnson told us how her father was the first Saban to drive a jeep, and she remembers the big event when a woman first drove on the island. What you do not learn during your first few hours on Saba, you can glean from *Saba: The First Guidebook*, an indispensable, thorough and chatty self-published booklet by Natalie and Paul Pfanstiehl (11 Annandale Road, Newport, RI 02840).

As you soon learn, Saba is known as "The Unspoiled Queen." Tourists have yet to discover this "green gumdrop" in significant numbers. The island's history, however, is marked by repeated discoveries, and battles for sovereignty — between the Dutch, English and French, with the Dutch taking final hold in 1816. Today, Dutch is the official language, but everyone speaks English. The Sabans, mostly descended from the original settlers and African slaves, take great pride in their island, keeping it strikingly clean and tidy. But they take great joy in sharing it as well.

What is there to do on a Caribbean island that rises so abruptly out of the sea that it has no beaches? The first thing is to explore the villages. Windwardside, on the ridge between Booby Hill and Mount Scenery, gives new depth to the adjective "charming." Stroll down narrow streets past the old churches and the graveyard, and wander through the handful of shops and stores: the Superette, the Island Craft Shop, and Big Rock Market. Browse through an eye-popping selection of colorful stamps at the Post Office (there are even more at the main Post Office in The Bottom). Pick up maps, postcards and information at the Tourist Office. At night, the activity is concentrated at the Chinese Restaurant, Guido's, where dancing takes precedence on the weekends, and Cousin's Bar. But the streets are quiet and you are serenaded to sleep by crickets, frogs, and the wind rustling through broad palm leaves.

It takes about an hour to walk from Windwardside down through St. John's and Crispeen to The Bottom, but if you wave for a ride, someone is sure to pick you up. (The taxi ride costs about $5.) In addition to several quaintly officious administrative buildings in The Bottom, you will find the Saba Artisan Foundation, selling the island's famous lace-like drawn needlework, T-shirts, and several varieties of Saba Spice, a sweet and potent homemade concoction of mulled 151-proof rum; Earl's Snack Bar, Saba's answer to fast food; the splendid little Corner View Bakery, selling breads, tarts and johnnycake; Nicholson's Supermarket; and the best native cooking on the island at Queenie's Serving Spoon.

After exploring Saba's "civilization," try the walks to Fort Bay or Ladder Bay from The Bottom; up Booby Hill or to the Lookout from Windwardside; a Botanical Tour with Anna Keene; or a walk up the challenging 1064 steps of Mt. Scenery, to an elevation of nearly 3000 feet. When you are ready for a swim, the lack of beaches is no obstacle: you can swim and snorkel off the pier at Fort Bay. If you scuba dive, you will quickly learn that Saba is one of the great unspoiled diving locales of the eastern Caribbean. Two diving facilities—Edward Arnold's Saba Deep, and Joan and Lou Bourque's Sea Saba —will assist you in exploring Saba's recently established Marine Park. Underwater visibility averages 75 to 125 feet, and at the two dozen or so dive spots you will find towering walls and pinnacles, giant coral mounds, sea fans, sponges, dense schools of fish and scores of crustaceans.

During our first afternoon and evening on Saba, we began to feel at home. After another day, we had caught on to the Saban courtesy of waving to everyone you meet on the road, and we made friends with Tipsy, the one-and-a-half-eared cat who jumps into your lap at Scout's Place. By the third day, we knew how hard it was going to be to leave this mountainous emerald paradise, and how easy it would be to return.

FAVORITE SPOTS

The hike up *MT. SCENERY*, via the 1064 stone steps, is steep and arduous at times. Most hikers average about an hour and 20 minutes to the top. But along the way you are rewarded with breathtaking views of all the settlements. The vegetation assumes giant proportions in the near rain forest setting. I sat for nearly an hour at the top, staring across the sea at St. Eustatius (Statia), and watching the clouds form and blow over the island as the cold sea air hit the warm air rising from the land.

The *SABA MUSEUM*, located near Captain's Quarters in Windwardside, was established in honor of Harry Luke Johnson, whose dream was to complete such a project. The memorabilia includes antique furniture, glassware, tools, and photographs and clippings relating the 20th-century history of Saba.

WHERE TO STAY
SCOUT'S PLACE
Windwardside, Saba, N.A.
Telephone: 599-4-2205

Scout's Place proves that paradise need not be expensive. Dianna
Medero manages five rooms and a homey one-bedroom apartment.
(A new wing of rooms was under construction in 1987.) The ginger-
bread-trimmed main building commands a gorgeous view of the
Caribbean, especially from the patio bar and outdoor dining room.
Dianna serves the island's best breakfast (bacon, eggs, fat slices of
homemade toast, juice, coffee or tea) in a cozy inside dining room
off the kitchen. In the late morning, several local residents and taxi
drivers gather at the bar for coffee and conversation. The kitchen
turns out hearty lunches and full course dinners. Rates are $50 double,
with breakfast and dinner included. (For a small extra charge, Dianna
will prepare lobster on special order.)

CAPTAIN'S QUARTERS
Windwardside, Saba, N.A.
Telephone: 599-4-2201

Perched on the verdant hillside below Scout's Place, Captain's Quarters is a beautifully restored former sea captain's home. Its ten rooms are neatly furnished, some with antique four-poster beds. The outdoor dining pavilion and terrace bar are vital centers of social activity, as is the swimming pool, unique among Saba's hotels. Full-course dinners feature lobster, steak, poultry or fish, and reservations are required. The hotel closes down for the month of September for maintenance. Rates are $75 (summer) and $95 (winter) double, plus room tax and service charge, with Modified American Plan available for $27 per person.

JULIANA'S APARTMENTS
Windwardside, Saba, N.A.
Telephone: 599-4-2269

Located right behind Captain's Quarters, these modern guest rooms (and a two-and-a-half room apartment) were built by Juliana Johnson, sister of Captain's Quarters' Steve Hassel. Each has private bath and a seaview balcony. Juliana's guests have use of the Captains Quarters' pool. Rates are $40 single, $50 double in the summer, $45 and $65 winter. The apartment is $65 summer, $95 winter.

CRANSTON'S ANTIQUE INN
The Bottom, Saba, N.A.
Telephone: 599-4-3208 or 3218

Originally built as a government guesthouse for visiting officials, this restored two-story Victorian house came under private management in 1964. J.C. Cranston and his son Edward have gradually turned the old building into a charming inn. The rooms are furnished with antiques and locally handcrafted curtains and coverlets. The tropical garden bar is a favorite afternoon and evening watering spot in The Bottom, and the recently completed dining gazebos provide romantic settings for meals. Rates are $70 double, breakfast included.

HOUSE AND APARTMENT RENTALS
A variety of cottages, apartments and houses in Hell's Gate, Windwardside, Booby Hill is available for daily, weekly and monthly rental, with rates ranging from $25 per day to $150 per week and $600 per month. The Saba Tourist Bureau maintains and publishes current listings. Telephone: 599-4-2231

RESTAURANTS
QUEENIE'S SERVING SPOON: "I have heart like marshmallow," Queenie Simmons told us when she was explaining the list of names on the wall: they were local Sabans who had not yet paid for meals she prepared on credit. Queenie and her daughters, Verna and Connie, also have a magic touch with the best, downhome West Indian cuisine on Saba. Located on a back street of The Bottom, Queenie's gaily painted and wildly decorated little cafe has eight tables beneath homemade crepe-paper "fly-catchers." For lunch, Queenie serves enormous portions of chicken in her special peanut butter sauce, with rice, greens and fresh french fries. Call ahead for dinner and she will prepare curried goat, stuffed onion fish, muffin dumplings, and banana or pumpkin fritters. She makes a dark, powerful Saba Spice as well. Her full-page typed receipts include the salutation, "So my loveing friends i am now thanking you all and please come back again be looking out for you all soon." The feeling is genuine, and mutual.

THE SABA CHINESE BAR AND RESTAURANT, in Windwardside, is famous for its egg rolls—but then it has little competition.

This Caribbean anomaly serves an extensive menu of Cantonese food and selected local dishes. At night, the bar often becomes crowded and raucous, and you can sometimes hear the music a block away.

GUIDO'S, behind the Post Office and the Library in Windwardside, serves pizza, made to order, all day. In the afternoon you can play a quiet game of darts, but at night the bar becomes a gathering spot for young Sabans and tourists, and the place jumps with dancers on the weekends.

HOW TO GET THERE

Pan Am, American and Eastern Airlines provide regular service to St. Maarten. Windward Air flies from St. Maarten to Saba three times a day. The flights are often booked solid, so be sure to reconfirm and check in early. The flight to Saba takes 15 minutes, unless a stop is added at Statia.

The speedboat Style makes the one hour trip three times a week from Phillipsburg, St. Maarten, to Saba, docking at Fort Bay.

NOTES

IMMIGRATION: A valid passport, birth certificate or alien registration card is required for entry, plus a return or onward transportation ticket.

CURRENCY: The official currency is the Netherlands Antilles Florin (or guilder), with an exchange rate of approximately 1.77 florins to the U.S. dollar. But U.S. currency is routinely accepted throughout the island.

BARBUDA

Paradise sometimes appears in the most peculiar and unexpected settings. Flying from Antigua to its sister island of Barbuda, one looks down on a rather uninviting landscape of flat, scrubby terrain. No rolling hills, winding rivers, spectacular cliffs or waterfalls beckon the airborne traveler descending to a forsaken-looking, waterbound patch of earth. But as the small plane eases down in an graceful arc toward the small landing strip at Codrington, the pink and white rim of the island starts to reveal Barbuda's very special story. For here, effectively removed from all the commercial trappings of a conventional Caribbean vacation, along the edge of 62 square miles of unremarkable land, are miles and miles of magnificent, unspoiled beaches—among the most beautiful and least exploited in the Caribbean, if not the world. Barbuda is so rich in sandy beaches that a sand exportation business sends the "excess" to larger Caribbean islands for construction and restoration of their more heavily touristed beaches. And yet only a few hundred visitors venture the 25 miles from Antigua each year to enjoy the breathtakingly idyllic pleasures of Barbuda's unspoiled coastal rim.

Also visible from the air are dark brown and grey patches that mottle the gorgeous azure sea surrounding the island. These are the shadows of coral reefs—acres of coral reefs that lie unexplored in Barbuda's shallow waters. So even before landing, you have glimpsed the unique appeal of this wonderfully undiscovered island.

At the two-room Barbuda airport, a dozen or so people await the arrival of each plane. We were greeted by George (a.k.a. Profit) Burton, the proprietor of the Sunset View Resort, ready to recruit guests for his nearby hotel. Later in the morning, George loaded us into his truck and provided a tour of the island. The road was exceptionally rough, pitted with ruts and holes, but George seemed to know every inch. He pointed out a coconut plantation, the Martelo tower, the sandloading operation. He accompanied us to Coco Point, past a sign that warned the driver to watch for low-flying aircraft. Less than a mile north of Coco Point, he pulled his truck over to a slight opening in the dense brush, and dropped us off at a gorgeous stretch of beach which we had to ourselves for the rest of the day. The sand was white and soft, and the calm waters had rock and coral formations within wading distance. Small fish circled around our ankles, practically playing tag with us as we swam. Like all the hosts on Barbuda, George Burton (one of many Barbudan Burtons) is a repository of information and tips, providing gracious hospitality and service to visitors. When we told him we had spotted a lobster underneath a rock ledge in the shallow waters, he told us we were very lucky. Indeed we were.

Barbuda is the ''lesser'' half of the two-island country Antigua-Barbuda, which gained its independence from Britain in 1983. Most of its 1300 black residents live in Codrington, a rustic village situated on the southeast side of the large Western or Codrington Lagoon. Birdwatchers will be fascinated by the great variety of species that nests on the island, especially at the Frigate Bird Sanctuary, accessible by private boat. Hunters occasionally roam through the brush inland or around the island's salt ponds in pursuit of wild boar, deer and duck. And if it is possible to tire of the absolute natural peace of sunning, swimming and snorkeling at any of the white sand and dazzling pink, shell-laden beaches, there are many landmarks to investigate such as the ruins of Sir William Codrington's Highland House estate, the Indian caves, or the Martello Tower, built by Spanish colonists as a beacon for ships at sea. Apparently, many seafarers

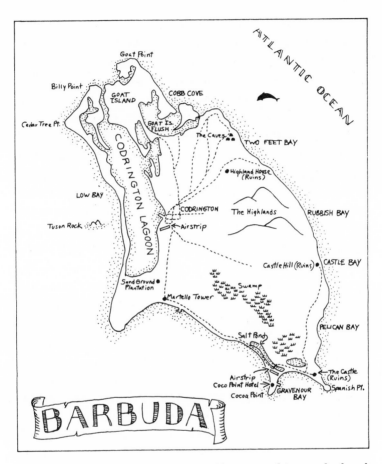

BARBUDA

did not spy the land in time, as some 60 or more ships crashed and sank in the Barbuda's shallow, reef-bound waters. The wrecks provide fascinating excursions for scuba divers.

I discovered one of Barbuda's most interesting social phenomena during a walk through Codrington at dusk. As George Burton later explained, every morning the village residents open their gates and let their small herds of goats roam and graze freely around the island. Around such public buildings as the school and Government House, the goats are used to mowing the wild grass into neat, closely cropped lawns. As sunset approaches, the goats migrate back to town in herds 100 or more strong. Once they reach the streets of Codrington, they break off into smaller groups and walk confidently through the neighborhood to find their own yard. It is an enlightening and moving experience to walk through the droves of tame, bleating goats as they are instinctively returning home. Once night falls, so does the level of activity in Codrington. This is not a tourist town. There are no souvenir shops or nightclubs, no dive shops or T-shirt concessions, just an eminently free and easy lifestyle for self-sufficient travelers who want to discover the best secluded Caribbean spots for themselves.

WHERE TO STAY
LE VILLAGE SOLEIL
Box 1104
St. John's, Antigua, West Indies
Telephone: (Canada): (418) 275-3861
Situated on one of the Barbuda's awesome south coast beaches, this casual resort is operated by French-speaking Canadians, Danie and Andre Cloutier. Their 16 rooms are situated in apartments and thatch-roof cottages, and they offer fine meals and such special excursions as lobster barbecues on the beach. Rates are $200-245 per day, modified American plan.

SUNSET VIEW RESORT
Belle Village, Barbuda, West Indies
Telephone: (809) 460-0078
Located about one-quarter mile outside Codrington, near the Lagoon, this 11-room, two-story hotel is the most comfortable, reasonably-priced accommodation on the island. Its simple and cozily modern

rooms are neatly appointed. The outdoor dining room and bar are especially attractive, in a garden setting surrounded by goat-mown fields. Rates are $40 single, $60 double.

COCO POINT LODGE
Box 90
St. Johns, Antigua, West Indies
Telephone: (809) 462-3816
Although Barbuda would not seem a likely setting for a luxury hotel, William Cody Kelly succeeded in establishing a stunning, country club-like resort on the southern coast of the island. Single-level cottages and bungalows are situated on their own secluded sections of one of the Caribbean's most beautiful palm-lined beaches. The grounds and gardens are immaculately groomed, and the main house dining room and cocktail terrace face a breathtaking expanse of sand and sea. Vacations here are expensive barefoot escapes. The ''all-inclusive'' rates, which range from $250 to $600 per day, provide for all food, drinks, the use of tennis courts, boats, snorkeling equipment and excursions.

GUEST HOUSES
The traveler on a more restricted budget will be able to find very basic accommodations in one of Codrington's several guest houses, including the THOMAS HOUSE (which sells specially-made postcards), located right next to the airport, and THE EARL'S, offering apartments and cottages in or near town. Detailed information is available from the Antigua-Barbuda Tourist Board in New York City: 610 5th Ave., Suite 311, New York, NY 10020. Telephone: (212) 541-4117.

NOTES
CURRENCY: Like Antigua, Barbuda uses the East Caribbean Dollar

(EC), with an exchange rate of approximately $2.60 EC to $1 U.S. There is a bank at the Antigua airport where you can exchange your money before flying on to Barbuda.

STAMPS: If you have a few extra minutes at the Antigua airport, stop at the Post Office near the bank window and browse through the beautiful Antigua-Barbuda postage stamps. They are printed in deliciously bright colors with pictures of fruits, flowers and wildlife.

HOW TO GET THERE
LIAT operates regularly scheduled morning and afternoon flights from Antigua to Barbuda.

MONTSERRAT

The natural beauty of Montserrat is abundantly evident as you fly in towards Blackburne Airport. The mountainous terrain is densely covered with dark green tropical foliage and forests. Misty clouds linger on the highest peaks. And the beauty only grows more intense as you get closer.

The warm hospitality of Montserrat is also abundantly evident as soon as you set foot in the tiny airport. The immigration officer asks where you are staying and offers his recommendations for lodging and car rentals, and will register you for a temporary driver's license after you have cleared customs. (It is best, however, to make your hotel decision on your own, after considering the options.) In the next room, the customs inspector hardly looks at your luggage; he is more interested in welcoming you to Montserrat. When he asks about the nature and extent of your visit, it seems less for official reasons than out of formal courtesy. And everything is accompanied by a smile.

Magnificent natural wonders and relaxed, informal hospitality are the key attractions of Montserrat, a 39-square-mile island 15 minutes by air from Antigua. It is an island of wonderful contrasts. Named by Christopher Columbus when he sailed by in 1493, Montserrat was first settled by Irish colonists (with a sprinkling of Scots and English) more than 350 years ago. The Irish influence is reflected in Montserrat's appropriate title as the "Emerald Island," in such place names as St. Patricks, Brodericks, Joe Morgan Hill and Galway Plantation, and in the Shamrock that is stamped onto your passport. But the

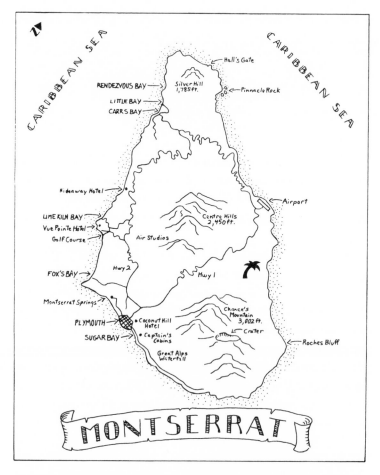

modern population of 13,000 is mostly black and English-speaking. The island has been visited by pop music superstars because of a world-famous recording studio, yet remains remarkably off-the-beaten track for most Caribbean tourists. It has a beautiful 100-acre golf course that seems anomalous amidst the vast expanses of lush unspoiled scenery. It is large enough to require auto transportation along its 115 miles of paved roads, but is best explored by foot from points where the roads end.

Plymouth is the main settlement, a partially rustic, partially modern village of 3000, located on the sheltered west coast of Montserrat. The drive from Blackburne Airport, on the east side, takes you along winding roads, through fertile farm land, past hundreds of grazing goats and cattle, up through the hills dotted with private homes, and back down to the Caribbean shore. In town, the narrow avenues are a maze of one-way streets, running past centuries-old buildings and churches and less interesting contemporary structures. Most visitors stay in or near Plymouth, taking advantage of the restaurants, car rentals, and easy access to the taxis that can carry you to the important sites north and south of town. During the day, the streets are busy, with people gathering in conversation on the corners. But at night, the town is still and looks virtually empty, especially in the summer season, with activity confined to the restaurants and pubs.

A hiker's paradise, with rewarding climbs and fascinating trails beckoning from all over the island, Montserrat cannot claim to be one of the Caribbean's best beach and diving locales. The waters are unpredictable, the coral reefs and coves few, and many of the beaches grey and pebbly. But the Caribbean side of the island has the gentlest and warmest water, with good snorkeling—at the best white sand beach near the Vue Point Hotel and at Rendezvous and Carr's Bay—and such interesting dives as The Pinnacle, off Woodlands Bay, and the Artificial Reef, where the government once dumped over 200 old cars into 80 feet of water near Fones Bay to attract sea life. Windsurfing is available at the Vue Point Hotel.

But here, in contrast to such beach-bound havens as Barbuda and the Bahamas, the water is almost an adjunct to the land. The possibilities for exploring the island are virtually limitless, from the exhilarating views from Old Fort on St. George's Hill, to the challenging climb up to the 3000 foot peak of Mount Chance. Most people return to Montserrat year after year, knowing that they can feel welcomed and immediately at home, yet always find something new to discover in the island's unique geographical splendor.

FAVORITE SPOTS

GREAT ALPS WATERFALL: We found a shortcut that reduced by at least half an hour the hiking time to this spectacular 70-foot waterfall, but we couldn't find our junction on the way back and thus added at least another 30 minutes to the walk to our car. So it is recommended that you either hire a guide or start from the main entrance near the southern end of the island. The walk is long and humid, but well worth the exertion. As you approach the falls, the ferns and other broad-leafed plants grow to enormous heights. They add to the spiritual feeling that mounts as you finally reach the waterfall, cascading down a sheer cliff into a small, slightly sulphurous pool. Take your time getting there, and consider carrying water and a picnic lunch or snack.

GALWAY'S PLANTATION: About a 15 or 20 minute drive south of Plymouth and up a winding ravine, the ruins of this 17th century sugar plantation are being meticulously excavated. A windmill, sugar boiling house and Great House are available for investigation. And the view that David Galway, an ambitious Irish plantation owner, commanded nearly 300 years ago has hardly changed.

GALWAY SOUFRIERE is the bubbling, sulfurous center of a volcano in the southern section of Montserrat, just up the hill from Galway's Plantation Estate. A fascinating 20-minute walk from the road's end takes you along rugged volcanic rock to the steaming sulfur vents.

FOX'S BAY BIRD SANCTUARY is located on the coast just north of Plymouth at Richmond Estate. Established as part of the Mont-

serrat National Trust in 1979, it is the nesting place of egrets, herons, cuckoos, kingfishers, coots and other species.

NOTEWORTHY
STAMPS: Although you might start off at the Plymouth Post Office looking for stamps, be sure someone directs you to the *PHILATELIC BUILDING* where you could spend hours perusing the marvelous stamps at the *MONTSERRAT STAMP SHOP*. The natural wonders of the island, from lizards and fish to the towering peaks, are depicted in vivid color. They are among the most beautiful and sought-after stamps in the Caribbean.

THE MONTSERRAT HISTORICAL SOCIETY MUSEUM is located in an old sugar mill near Richmond Hill, and houses exhibits reflecting the natural and cultural history of the island, and a fascinating postage stamp collection.

AIR STUDIOS: Rock stars from all over the world, including Stevie Wonder, Elton John, Paul McCartney and Sting, have traveled to Montserrat to record at the famous Air Studios, secluded on the outskirts of Plymouth. Although they are closed to the public, you may request a tour of the sophisticated facilities by calling studio manager Yvonne Kelly for an appointment. Telephone: (809) 491-5678

WHERE TO STAY
VUE POINTE HOTEL
P.O. Box 65
Olde Towne, Montserrat, W.I.
Telephone: (809) 491-5210
The Vue Pointe has a widespread reputation as Montserrat's finest

and friendliest hotel, to which many guests return year after year. But it is also the most expensive. Its 16 rooms and 24 hexagonal cottages are scattered among palm trees on spacious, neatly groomed grounds. Located next to Montserrat's beautiful Belham Valley Golf Course, it has a swimming pool with a spectacular sea view, and is only about 100 yards from one of the island's best beaches. The special Wednesday night barbecue with live steel band music is a popular event. Rates are $135-185 for a double during winter, Modified American Plan, and $55-80 summer EP (with Modified American Plan available for $30 per person).

COCONUT HILL
P.O. Box 337
Plymouth, Montserrat, W.I.
Telephone: (809) 491-2144
This picturesque, woodframe building is a short walk from both town and nearby Sugar Bay Beach. Its nine rooms are tastefully appointed with antique furniture, and all have splendid balcony views of either the sea or the verdant hillsides. West Indian cuisine is served in a charming dining room that opens out on a fantastic vista of the sea. Rates are $66-92 for a double in winter and $48-78 summer, depending on your choice of meal plan.

WADE INN
Parliament St.
Plymouth, Monserrat, W.I.
Telephone: (809) 491-2881
Conveniently situated in the middle of town, the Wade Inn offers very basic accommodations. Compared to the hillside and seaview hotels, its location is rather mundane although it makes Plymouth immediately accessible. Reasonable prices and a restaurant that is considered one of the finest in town greatly enhance its appeal. There is dancing

to live music on Friday nights. Rates are $35 single and $47 double, with MAP available.

APARTMENT AND VILLA RENTALS
Weekly and monthly rentals are available in Plymouth and its outlying areas. For information, contact the DEPARTMENT OF TOURISM, P.O. Box 7, Plymouth, Montserrat, W.I. Telephone: (809) 491-2230

RESTAURANTS
THE PANTRY, in Plymouth, is a casual restaurant that is very good for breakfast and lunch home-cooking.

THE ATTIC, upstairs in the same building as The Pantry, is popular for its homey cuisine and breezy rooftop dining with a superb view.

THE IGUANA, at the edge of Plymouth, in Wapping, combines an informal setting with a mixed menu of unusual items such as fried Camembert, pizza and pates. Student parties are sometimes rowdy, but a separate garden patio offers escape out back.

WONG GEE CAT, still sometimes called Chez Nous, is located in Plymouth, upstairs behind Ram's Market, and serves excellent West Indian and Chinese food.

THE OASIS, in Plymouth, next door to the Plantation Club, is renowned for its "mountain chicken," a euphemism for giant frog legs.

HOW TO GET THERE
LIAT, BWIA and Montserrat Air have regularly scheduled flights from Antigua to Blackburne Airport on the northeast coast of Montserrat.

NOTES

IMMIGRATION: A valid passport or proof of identity is required for entry, plus a return or onward transportation ticket.

CURRENCY: The currency on Montserrat is the Eastern Caribbean dollar (EC), with an exchange rate of approximately $2.60 EC to one US dollar.

FRENCH WEST INDIES

MARIE-GALANTE

It is an enigma that an island as large as Marie-Galante, with such superb beaches and even a unique ocean-front hotel, can be so undiscovered. Rarely will you find more than a handful of visitors. Even at Christmas, while other islands are packed to capacity, the beaches on Marie-Galante are relatively empty. The only possible explanation is that barely a word of English is spoken anywhere on the island. For the intrepid traveler who does not mind the challenge of a French-speaking island not geared to tourism, the rewards are many.

The trip from Pointe-a-Pitre, Guadeloupe, is an easy one, either by ferry (one hour) or by air (ten minutes, landing on the flat plain a few miles south of Grand-Bourg). Coming immediately into view are the sugar cane fields and idle 19th-century stone windmills. Grand-Bourg, a town of 10,000 inhabitants, is a busy scene of ugly concrete structures mixed with more interesting wooden buildings. The balconies over the sidewalks are similar to those in the Latin Quarter of New Orleans, and there is a covered outdoor market where colorfully dressed women sell spices, fruit, vegetables and clothing.

To explore the island beyond the principal town of Grand-Bourg (pronounced in patois as "GAM-bo"), ten-passenger minibuses can be hailed like taxis all day from 6 a.m. to 5 p.m. You get off anywhere along the route and pay the 5F tariff as you exit. As you ride along the ocean front road to the smaller towns of St. Louis and Capesterre, there is the temptation to stop as each beach becomes progressively more inviting. Snorkeling at Capesterre is excellent, and from here it is a very long swim or a short walk to "les Galeries," massive and impressive rock formations that have been carved out by the surf. Continuing inland, "Trou a Diable" is a magnificent cave for the adventurous. It is some 550 yards long with an underground lake. Safer, perhaps, is the marvelous walk along the cliff-fringed coast with its rocky promontories and secluded coves to "Caye Plate," a steep-sided crag with extensive views, where local fisherman catch crayfish of exceptional size.

Marie-Galante is a delight to explore. Each turn of the coast offers another marvelous vista, secluded cove, or immense stretch of

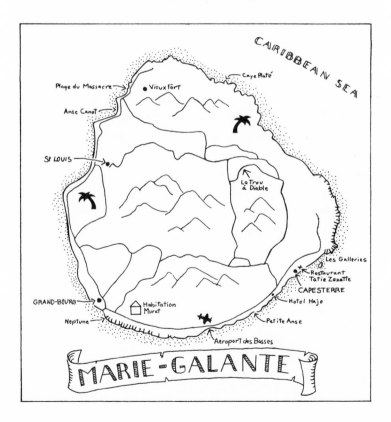

quiet beach. Staying here is like returning to another era, before the tourism boom of the 1950s covered most islands with highrise hotels and curio shops.

WHERE TO STAY
HOTEL HAJO
97140 Capesterre
Marie-Galante via Guadeloupe
No telephone
Mediterranean in style with unusual sculpture and furniture, each of the six rooms at Hotel Hajo faces the sea. Hajo is an amazing place. Rarely will you see another guest, except at Christmas when the total number might rise to 12. Food is French and Creole, excellent and hearty, served on the seaside veranda. The location could not be better: it is a ten-minute walk to the village of Capesterre or a five-minute walk to one of the best beaches on the island. How Hotel Hajo can stay in operation with rates as low as $36 per day for two, offering accommodations with private bath, in a fine seaside location, is just another enigma of Marie-Galante.

AUBERGE DE LA ROCHE D'OR
Capesterre
Marie-Galante via Guadeloupe, French West Indies
Telephone: (590) 97-91-92
This small, basic inn is across the road from a good beach. Inexpensive.

HOTEL SOLEDAD
Section Pyrogue
Grand-Bourg, Marie-Galante via Guadeloupe, French West Indies
Telephone: (590) 97-75-45

Set in a garden with a sea view, this is a large house with 20 spartan rooms (eight are air conditioned). Its restaurant features creole specialties. Rates are $38 for two.

RESTAURANTS
TATIE ZEZETTE, Plage La Feuillere, Capesterre, offers very good creole cuisine with vintage wine. The owner is charming, but you must speak French. Telephone 97-96-84.

NEPTUNE, Rue Beaurenon ze Pont, Grand-Bourg, offers delicious jambon pizza and reasonable French seafood dishes, including *mousseline de poisson, langoustes, coquille d'oursins gratinees, darne de daurade au poivre vert*, and wood-grilled fish and meat. Telephone 97-96-90.

CHEZ HENRI ET BAPTISTE, in Saint Louis, is a very charming, intimate restaurant with excellent food. But here, as at all restaurants on Marie-Galante, you should give them an hour's notice before you arrive so they can turn on the generator and buy the food. Since there are literally no tourists, each restaurant will be your own private dining room. No telephone.

NOTEWORTHY
HABITATION MURAT is a Baroque-style plantation manor built in the 18th century and destroyed by earthquake in 1843. It is now a museum with sea life exhibits. The restored windmill is the most fascinating building on the estate grounds, and from the tower there are commanding views of Dominica.

VIEUX-FORT, an old-world village on a fine beach, is a fascinating collection of pile dwellings which were common all over the island until the 19th century.

FAVORITE SPOTS

PLAGE DU MASSACRE is a fine, long beach with many excellent picnic spots beneath shady trees. This is a quieter, less populated part of the island.

ST. LOUIS, a town of 4000 inhabitants, is worth exploring on foot. The old, weathered stores and houses on the back streets are infinitely more interesting than the new concrete building of Capesterre and Grand-Bourg. Along the waterfront, multicolored fishing boats glisten on the clear, calm sea in the bright sun. A fine beach is just minutes to the north by foot.

NOTES FROM MY JOURNAL

What an adventure renting a car tonight! The owner had never seen an American driver's license and perused both sides with gleeful amazement. No deposit, no contract. Total faith and trust in this visitor from another planet. I drove off into the unexplored darkness, happy to have landed on ''an island in time.''

TERRE DE HAUT

One Caribbean island is so ideal that the visitor has to wonder why few people other than Jacques Cousteau have discovered it and made it their home. Its striking terrain, panoramic vistas, empty, breathtaking beaches and dazzling water, gracious population, fine cuisine and refreshing paucity of tourism all conspire to make it a genuine paradise. If its dependence on rain for drinking water did not inhibit future development, I would be reluctant to even divulge the name of this, one of my very favorite islands. Fortunately, Terre de Haut will remain relatively unspoiled as it can sustain only a small number of visitors at any one time.

"Iles des Saintes" is a tiny cluster of islands seven miles off the southwestern tip of Guadeloupe. Terre de Haut (more often referred to as les Saintes) is the archipelago's island metropolis although it is less than six square miles in size with fewer than 5000 inhabitants. It is the only island with several choices of accommodation.

The beaches on les Saintes are marvelous; swimming and snorkeling are excellent. But that is only one small part of this island's appeal. Because the remarkable hilly terrain of les Saintes is unsuited for agriculture, the French never colonized the islands for anything but strategic reasons. There was no plantation system and thus, no history and no legacy of slave labor. The peaceful relationship between the French and the native *Santois* has resulted in a minimum of racial tension and economic disparity. Poverty, unemployment and crime are unknown here; there isn't even a jail.

Of the mere dozen vehicles on the island, most are taxi vans serving as transport to and from the airport, for school outings to the beach, or occasionally as an ambulance. The narrow concrete roads thus become extrawide "sidewalks" where you can stroll leisurely without the intrusion of motor traffic. One can walk easily anywhere on the island in less than an hour.

Terre de Haut is the island's major town. A picturesque little settlement of small, red-roofed houses, it is centrally located on a curving bay between the hills. These charming houses and stores are spotlessly clean and beautifully adorned with colorful vines and a myriad of flowers in dozens of pots and jars. This is not a town reconstructed for the sake of tourism; it is a neatly maintained fishing village where life revolves around the sea. Purple, pink and mauve fishing nets are used to haul in the daily catch. What is not consumed in private homes behind 18th century doors is sold to the local restaurants. Terre de Haut hosts frequent weekend visitors from Guadeloupe who enjoy fine dining at the many small restaurants along the waterfront and back streets. The cuisine of les Saintes is French and creole and consistently superb.

WHERE TO STAY
HOTEL BOIS JOLI
Terre de Haut, Les Saintes
via Guadeloupe, F.W.I.
Telephone: (509) 99-50-38
Not known for its friendly management, and difficult for non-French speaking visitors, this 21-room hotel has a very private location along the coast one mile from town. The rooms are spartan but comfortable, the choicest being those on the top floor with incredible views, and the three beachfront bungalows. Swimming is excellent and the snorkeling is outstanding at the far end of the beach. You can walk

or ride the taxi van into town, but the Hotel also operates a small boat into town three times daily for about $1 each way. About halfway on the very pleasant, scenic ride you will pass Jacques Cousteau's private cove. Rates at Bois Joli start at $92.00 double, including breakfast and dinner.

JEANNE d'ARC
Terre de Haut, Les Saintes
via Guadeloupe, F.W.I.
Telephone: (509) 99-50-41

This small ten-room beachfront hotel is situated at the end of the village, within walking distance of the town's plaza, wharf and restaurants. The best rooms face the beach and rent for approximately $20 nightly per person (when the franc-to-dollar exchange rate was 8 to 1). The beach front dining room serves excellent food.

HOUSEKEEPING ACCOMMODATIONS

LA COLLINE
Terre de Haut, Les Saintes
via Guadeloupe, F.W.I.
Telephone: (509) 99-52-19
Each of these five bungalows has a small kitchen and a magnificent view of the harbor and Fort Napoleon above that. They are a three minute walk from a beach, five minutes from town, and 30 minutes from the island's best and largest beach.

AUBERGE DES ANACARDIERS
La Savane, Terre de Haut
Les Saintes, Guadeloupe, F.W.I.
Telephone: (509) 95-09-90
You can be assured the warmest welcome on the island at this charming, 10-room wood chalet with swimming pool that overlooks the harbor. This is the newest addition to the island's accommodations, and the owners are trying very hard to please their guests. Secluded and quiet, Anacardiers is just a very short walk to the town or beach. Breakfast and a superb dinner are included in the daily rate of 550 francs for two. ($95)

Joelle et Jean-Claude Martin
MAISON IRENEE

Grande Ravine
97190 Gosier
Guadeloupe, F.W.I.
Telephone: (509) 26-72-63
This French Canadian couple on Guadeloupe rents out an inexpensive studio in Terre de Haut.

If you chat with the local residents, you might be able to find a room in a private house, "chez l'habitant." Ask shopkeepers or consult the detailed list at the town hall.

CAMPING
Camping is allowed at the Pont-Pierre beach, one of the most beautiful undeveloped bays in the Caribbean.

LOCAL CUISINE
It is probably impossible to get a bad meal from any of the dozen or so small restaurants on les Saintes. The beach front dining room at Hotel Jean d'Arc also has noteworthy cuisine. Among the local delicacies are: *crabes farcis*, stuffed crab; *accra*, a small fritter of cod or malanga root; *daube de lambis*, a conch stew; *blaff*, made with fish or sea urchins; *ragout de chartrous*, small octopus served with red beans; *poulet a la noix de coco*, local free-range chicken cooked in coconut milk. Desserts include *bananes flambe* and the les Saintes specialty, *tourment d'amour*, coconut tarts, often sold on the streets by the island's incredibly beautiful, blond children.

FAVORITE SPOTS
PAIN DU SUCRE: The tiny, exquisitely beautiful double-cove at Pain du Sucre is hard to find. In fact, I only discovered it on my second

visit when some local residents asked the taxi-van to stop on my way back to Hotel Bois Joli. Carrying towels and snorkeling gear, they disappeared suddenly on the steep path beneath the road. Their destination was this marvelous hidden spot, where snorkeling is excellent. And, should you become thirsty or hungry, there is even a small, informal beach restaurant. To get here from town, ask the taxi-van for Pain du Sucre, or take the Bois Joli boat and, for an extra few francs, ask them to stop. By foot, you can reach the cove through a hilly, 40-minute walk from town.

PONT PIERRE BEACH: Totally protected by cliffs, this unspoiled, undeveloped bay is one of the most beautiful in the Caribbean. Visitors from Guadeloupe come on the weekends for the fine snorkeling and swimming, but even then it is hardly overcrowded. Limited camping is available for a nominal fee.

FORT NAPOLEON: Built at the beginning of the 19th century to replace an earlier 17th century fort, Fort Napoleon contains a small museum. The 30-minute walk is pleasant and the views make the climb worthwhile.

MORNE DU CHAMEAU: At 1014 feet, this is the highest point on the island. From the top you can enjoy breathtaking panoramic views of Guadeloupe to the north, Marie-Galante to the east, and Dominca to the south.

HOW TO GET THERE

There are regular 15-minute flights ($16 one-way) from Basse Terre and Point-a-Pitre on Guadeloupe. By sea, regular ferry service is offered from Trois-Rivieres on Guadeloupe (with less regular trips from Basse Terre).

SPECIAL NOTES

Since there are few hotels on les Saintes, it is important to have a reservation in the peak seasons, December 15-March 15, Bastille Day (July 14) and Liberation Day (August 15-17).

Take a flashlight, as the roads are not lit at night, and on moonless nights the countryside beyond town is pitch dark.

IMMIGRATION: a passport is required, but no visa.

TERRE DE BAS

The other inhabited island of Iles des Saintes, Terre de Bas, is only three miles from Terre de Haut but is remarkably separate. Because there is no regular boat service, this small island is rarely visited. But now that overnight lodging is available, Terre de Bas is well worth exploring. A walker's paradise, crisscrossed with scenic hiking trails and small one-lane roads, the island can be explored at the leisurely pace found only on such undiscovered spots.

The road begins at the ferry landing at Anse des Muriers. Just a few hundred yards inland, at the first fork in the road, you encounter Arlette's Restaurant, a source of good food and valuable information about the island. The small road to the left leads to Grande Anse, a tiny village clustered around a primitive 17th century church. Swimmers and snorkelers will want to take this detour to Grande Anse and enjoy refreshing drinks at the beachside *"lolos."*

Back on the main cross-island road past Arlette's, each bend offers a different and more spectacular view before the final descent into Petites Anses. Island life is focused here around the town hall, post office, fire station, dispensary, school, church, cemetery, hotel and restaurant. Next to the marina, colorful Santois fishing boats line the beach and fishing nets dry in the warm sun.

WHERE TO STAY
HOTEL LE POISSON-VOLANT

Petites Anses, Terre de Bas
Iles de Saintes
via Guadeloupe, F.W.I.
Telephone: (509) 99-8047

The only hotel in town has nine rooms. Rates: approximately $40 per night, depending on the French franc exchange rate.

It is possible to rent a room with meals at Chez Renaud Vala or Chez Arlette (telephone (509)-99-8166). A knowledge of French is almost

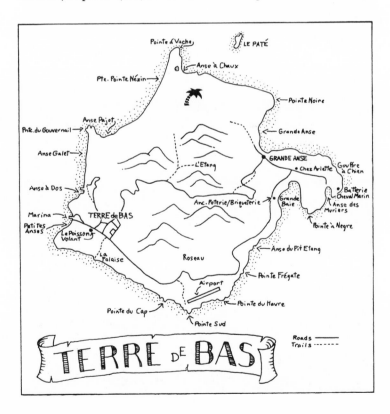

essential on Terre de Bas, unless you are confident that you can get by with mime and sign language.

HOW TO GET THERE

Irregular ferry service is available from Basse Terre on Guadeloupe, most likely on Monday, Wednesday, Thursday and Saturday, departing at 12:30 p.m. and arriving at Terre de Bas two hours later. On the boat, ask about return sailing times and days. If your French is good, you can arrange for a local fisherman to take you from Terre de Haut, where there is regular air and boat service to Guadeloupe.

THE GRENADINES

The Grenadine Islands are simply sensational; there are over 120 of them in the 50 miles between St. Vincent and Grenada, but only 11 are inhabited. They are a boat-owner's paradise: very tropical, hilly islands with many fine harbors and coves, constant breezes, charming villages, friendly people, and superb, uncrowded beaches.

The most beautiful and undiscovered of the inhabited islands are now accessible to anyone willing to make the effort to get there. Several of the islands have small airports, and there is local boat service to the others.

Starting at the top in the St. Vincent Grenadines, Bequia is a well-discovered international destination. It is a beautiful island with many fine small hotels and excellent beaches. Loyal visitors return year after year to this friendly island, accessible only by boat from St. Vincent. Mustique has marvelous beaches and coves and attracts an international crowd to Cotton House and the island's 50 private houses which give this pleasant island its celebrity status. To the south, Canouan never has more than two dozen visitors at any one time; there are just two small beach front hotels, a handful of cars and 700 hospitable people. Not far away, Mayreau is a return to another century, so undiscovered that no one on Carriacou (ten miles away) knew if there were any inhabitants or any place to spend the night! Spectacular Union Island, with two lofty peaks rising from the aquamarine sea, has its share of yachts but still remains quiet and friendly. Here also are Petit St. Vincent, Palm Island and Young Island, the three privately-owned and fairly well publicized resort islands of the Grenadines.

Crossing the border from the St. Vincent Grenadines to the Grenada Grenadines, Petit Martinique and Carriacou bring the total number to five exceptional, undiscovered jewels in the Grenadine crown: Canouan, Mayreau, Union, Petit Martinique and Carriacou.

CARRIACOU

Carriacou's 13 square miles of towering hill and white sand beaches make it the largest and most populated of the Grenadines. It is also one of the most beautiful and certainly the most interesting. On this rich agricultural island, the Scots settled in Windward, the French in L'Esterre, and the English in Hillsborough, leaving an influence still in evidence today. This European heritage mixes with descendants of black slaves who have preserved many old cultural and spiritual traditions resembling the Xango of Trinidad and the voodoo cult of Haiti.

In the town of Windward, villagers of Scottish descent carry on the tradition of building wooden schooners from local white cedar. Skeletons of boats in various stages of completion are often seen on the beach where workers use centuries-old techniques and rudimentary tools to create the West Indian trade schooner fleet. Many of the Windward boats sail in the Carriacou Regatta held during the first weekend in August. It is a wonderful time to visit, as the island's 8000 inhabitants celebrate on land as well as sea.

The sounds of conga drums fill the air and all eyes turn toward the dancers who celebrate the harvest of the land and sea with dances handed down over generations. The people of Carriacou remember the African tribes from which they came—Congo, Moko, Mandinka, Ibo, Kromanti—and their dances are spectacular. The island's four-day festivities also include swimming, model boats, ball games, tug-of-war, and everyone's favorite, greasy pole.

By Wednesday, Hillsborough town has returned to its normal level of activity. With a population of just under 900, there are few traffic jams, no stoplights and no need to hurry. Main street parallels the beach. Built of stone and shingle, many of the stores have fascinating names: the Industrious Store, the Family Store (a good place to buy stamps), Morning Star Bakery, No Trust, Trust is to Burst, and No Hell. Near the pier are the post office, the fruit and vegetable market, and the government customs office.

Leaving the town and heading north into the hills toward Wind-

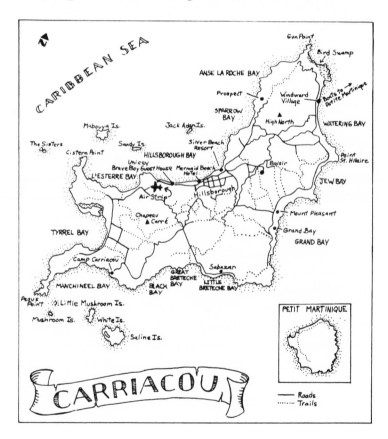

ward, the nature lover will delight in the flora and fauna of this lush, tropical island. Bougainvillea and flamboyants flourish and there are many varieties of cactus. Sugar apples, papayas, and limes are abundant. Dogwood and White Immortelle are two trees in Carriacou unknown in Grenada. The Southern Mockingbird, the Antillean Grackle and the Banaquit are the most common birds (the Banaquit is in the yellow phase, which is rare in Grenada). Among others to be seen are glossy cowbirds, ramiers, ground doves, wood doves, kingbirds, elaenias, emerald throated hummingbirds, and frigate birds. Not often seen but occasionally heard is the mangrove cuckoo.

WHERE TO STAY
SILVER BEACH RESORT
Carriacou, Grenada, West Indies
Telephone: (809) 443-7337
Local islanders, the Bullen family, own and manage this small, friendly resort. There are four duplex cottages (some with kitchens) facing the dining area and beach. Your waitress will most likely be singing when she carries your breakfast to your front veranda. The swimming is excellent in front of the hotel and to the left it is a five minute walk to the center of Hillsborough town. On the right, at the end of the beach, is a footpath that rises above the beach and hugs the coastline for a very pleasant walk at sunset. Rates start at $65 single and $80 double.

THE MERMAID BEACH HOTEL
Hillsborough, Carriacou, Grenada, West Indies
Telephone: (809) 443-7484
Formerly a private house, The Mermaid Inn is now an 11-room beach front inn on the opposite edge of town from Silver Beach Resort. Some of the rooms have four-poster beds and overlook a small courtyard

where meals are served on the water's edge. The staff is very pleasant, and your fellow visitors are often down-islanders from Grenada. Rates are $40 single and $50 double.

PROSPECT LODGE
Carriacou, Grenada, West Indies
Telephone: (809) 443-7380

On a hill 200 yards above the sea, and on the edge of a proposed national park, Prospect is restful and quiet. Lee and Ann Katzenbach offer comfortable and very moderately priced accommodations, good food, a library, snorkel gear, binoculars, small locally made boats, helpful advice and local guides. A room for two overlooking the garden with shared bath is $25. The apartment, a self-contained unit with bedroom, kitchen, bath and a private porch with the best view, is $40 single, $45 double. Orchard Cottage, in a separate building, has two bedrooms, kitchen and bath, and is $60 for two to four guests, $45 for one or two.

Meals: Breakfast and dinner are $14 a day. Picnic lunches are gladly packed. (A 20% government tax is charged on all meals.)

UNICEY BRAVEBOY
Lauriston, Carriacou, Grenada, West Indies
Telephone: (809) 443-7471

For the traveler on a budget, Unicey Braveboy runs a guesthouse in Lauriston, facing the quiet road and beach. There is a communal bathroom and kitchen, and rates begin at $18 per day.

MELONIE'S VILLA
Windward Village, Carriacou
Telephone (809) 443-7227, New York (718) 493-5383

This unpretentious stone villa is actually two buildings that can accommodate eight people. The dining/living room is enormous and

has one of the most spectacular views in the Caribbean: Petit Martinique, Petit St. Vincent and Union Islands in the distance. A native of Carriacou, Andrew Fleary lives in New York but returns to his house as often as he can save the airfare to do so. In the interim, he rents both buildings for $450 a week, which includes maid service.

NOTE: When writing for reservations, keep in mind that mail can take two weeks in each direction.

RESTAURANTS

TIP TOP RESTAURANT AND BAR, on Main Street, is known for its good local dishes.

ROOF GARDENS RESTAURANT AND BAR faces the jetty and market, featuring seafood and local foods.

L'AQUILONE BAR AND RESTAURANT serves homemade fettucini, lasagna and pizza.

FAVORITE SPOTS

SANDY ISLAND, just off Carriacou, is a wonderful place for snorkeling and picnicking. Other nearby islets are the Sisters, Mabouya, and Jack-A-Dan.

CARRIACOU MUSEUM, on a side street off Main in Hillsborough, has an interesting collection of Amerindian and European artifacts. Small and friendly, this little museum is a rarity for such a small island.

TYRREL BAY, on the west side, is a spectacular enclosed bay where the water is always calm and serene. Paradise Beach is a favorite for local residents and the swimming here is excellent.

HOW TO GET THERE

LIAT flies from Barbados and Grenada, and inter-island boats travel from St. Vincent and Grenada. Alexia II leaves St. Georges on Grenada at 10 a.m. on Wednesday and Saturday, and returns from Hillsborough wharf at 10 a.m. on Monday and Thursday.

PETIT MARTINIQUE

The extinct volcanic peak of Petit Martinique rises dramatically from the sea, a beckoning Bali Hai to those on nearby Carriacou. From the village of Windward, it is easy to arrange a boat for the 30 minute, three-mile trip across varying shades of blue water to the reef-protected island.

Veralyn "Ann" Jones, a beautiful and intelligent lady from New York, joined me on the boat trip to Petit Martinique. For her, this first visit was extremely special. Her father, John Jones, was born on this quiet island of 600 industrious black inhabitants.

On arrival, the beach was a hub of boating activity — painting, polishing and other last-minute preparations for the annual regatta. There are no paved roads and no cars on the island, so it was easy to discover this beautiful and quiet island by foot.

FAVORITE SPOT
The hike to the top of Petit Martinique's highest peak affords a spectacular view of the surrounding islands: Petit St. Vincent, Carriacou, Union, Canouan, and several uninhabited islands.

WHERE TO STAY
MRS. PETROILLA CAESAR
Petit Martinique via Carriacou, Grenada, West Indies
No telephone

UNION ISLAND

The flight from Carriacou to Union Island takes just five minutes, barely time to marvel at the islands below: Petit Martinique, Petit St. Vincent, and Palm Island. The landing over the harbor town of Clifton, with white sailboats shining on the glimmering azure sea, is spectacular; it passes so quickly that you long for a slow-motion rerun.

The picturesque airport building is an international arrival point to the St. Vincent Grenadines, but rarely do more than two or three passengers enter here from neighboring Carriacou in the Grenada Grenadines. The immigration officer is delighted to see a new arrival to his island, and with passport shown and duly stamped, the visitor is free to leave. The unusual, mountainous beauty of Union is immediately overwhelming.

The plane has departed for Mustique, and the stillness of the island adds to the allure of its tropical remoteness. Mount Taboi rises to 1000 feet on one side, and to the other is the sea. This could easily be Tahiti! But here on Union there is no traffic, there are no screeching motorbikes, no buses, no taxis. It is Tahiti before Gauguin. A grassy path lined with conch shells shows the way across the runway to the Anchorage Hotel. From there along the waterfront and beach, it is a five minute walk to Clifton town, comprised of several general stores, markets, a minuscule tourist office, two small, locally owned hotels, a few bars and restaurants, and shops selling local handicrafts.

Union Island is a hiker's paradise. The walks are many and all are

Roads ——————
Trails ----------

UNION ISLAND

rewarding. Crossing the island to the north are Richmond Bay and Belmont Bay. The English-speaking inhabitants along the way are friendly, as are the ubiquitous, well-behaved brown goats.

Asked for the third time if I were a priest, I facetiously answered in Latin, thus establishing my reputation for my one remaining day on Union Island. On inquiry I learned it was not my round glasses, white shirt, or Panama hat; it was my manner of rushing around with important business to do! Hilarious visions of Jacques Tati on Union Island came to mind. I decided it was time to move more leisurely and less conspicuously on to the next island.

NOTEWORTHY

CHATHAM BAY, is a beautiful and sequestered bay on the East Coast, with excellent swimming.

FRIGATE ISLAND, part of the Lagoon Reef which protects almost the entire South coast, is an ideal place for snorkeling.

WHERE TO STAY

ANCHORAGE YACHT CLUB
Clifton, Union Island
St. Vincent Grenadines
Telephone: (809) 458-8244

The five rooms in a coconut grove facing the sea are extremely comfortable, and another five are upstairs in the main building overlooking the tasteful outdoor dining area. This is a French-owned hotel and the clientele is international and "assez chic." Scuba lessons and

equipment are available. Rates are $50 single and $75 for two in low season.

SUNNY GRENADINES HOTEL
Clifton, Union Island
St. Vincent Grenadines
Telephone: (809) 458-8327
King Mitchell, a retired Union Island seaman, welcomes travelers to his informal waterfront hotel set in a quiet garden. The duplex units facing the sea are the ones to request. Mr. Mitchell is happy to arrange inexpensive boat trips to Tobago Cays (excellent snorkeling) and neighboring islands. Rates start at $40 single and $50 for two.

CLIFTON BEACH HOTEL
Clifton, Union Island
St. Vincent Grenadines
Telephone: (809) 458-8235
There are ten rooms with private baths facing the beach of Clifton town harbor. The rooms are spartan but comfortable, and the staff is friendly. Clifton Beach Hotel is owned by a local islander, Conrad Adams. Rates start at $25 single and $35 double.

Travelers on a tight budget will be warmly welcomed at the Clifton Beach Guest House in Clifton Town.

HOW TO GET THERE
There is air service on LIAT from Barbados, St. Vincent, Grenada and Carriacou, and on Air Martinique to points north, St. Vincent, Dominica and Martinique. Local boat from St. Vincent leaves at 10 a.m. on Monday and Thursday and returns on Tuesday and Friday (see ferry schedule at the end of the Grenadines chapter.)

NOTE: Save money for the departure tax when you leave Union (St. Vincent Grenadines) for Carriacou (Grenada Grenadines).

MAYREAU

The 100 inhabitants of quiet Mayreau are devout Roman Catholic and I was grateful to have preceded my own "priestly" reputation. Dropped off as the sole passenger of the sailing vessel United Knowledge, I walked slowly up the path away from the beach. I felt the centuries dissolve as the "United Knowledge" disappeared around a distant point and I was alone to discover the tranquil beauty of the island. Mayreau is small, only one-and-a-half square miles, yet on foot it seems much larger. There are no roads and no cars. There are only goats, sheep, virgin beaches, the land and the sea.

Life on Mayreau revolves around the sea, fishing and sailing. The wooden houses are small but not without character, and many have small subsistence vegetable gardens. A true sense of community pervades the island. Everyone meets for mass in the charming stone Catholic church with its magnificent view. In this very quiet, rural island existence, no one goes without if help is needed. Rarely will you see another person on the beaches, except perhaps a fisherman or occasionally a visiting yachtsman who has anchored in Salt Whistle Bay. To stay overnight or for a few days offers an experience rarely felt in the 20th century.

NOTEWORTHY
The walk across the island's lowland to the windward side is worth taking. In the dry season there are intricate crystals of rock salt in what was a salt pond, and on the beach one can find shells and interesting driftwood.

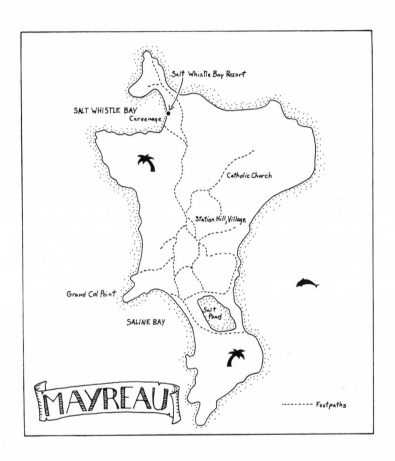

WHERE TO STAY
SALT WHISTLE BAY
Mayreau via Union Island
St. Vincent Grenadines
Radio phone: VHF CH 16
Salt Whistle Bay provides the island's only overnight accommodations, a low-key resort hidden among the trees on the beach facing Salt Whistle Bay. Rates start at $40 single and $50 double.

CANOUAN

Waiting for the small launch to arrive for the move from schooner to shore, one can tell even before setting foot on Canouan that it is a beachlover's paradise. On this quiet island, the beaches are long, empty and incredibly white against the calm turquoise sea.

On shore, the island is brown and rather barren in the lowland, and yet very green and tropical on the hills. The jungle casts its shadow on the end of Grand Bay and turns the water an emerald green for a never-to-be-forgotten swim at sunset.

Fishing, farming and sailing occupy most of the island's 700 shy but friendly English-speaking inhabitants. The roads are not paved, and only very occasionally will you need to step aside for a passing jeep.

WHERE TO STAY
CRYSTAL SANDS HOTEL
Canouan, St. Vincent, Grenadines
No telephone
The hospitable La Roches, native of Canouan, own and manage this five duplex cottage resort. The rooms are very basic, each with private bath and paper-thin walls. But if you get one of the three cottages directly on the beach, you will be so entranced with the location, the excellent swimming and friendly fellow guests (usually islanders from St. Vincent) that any inconvenience will quickly be forgotten. Rates

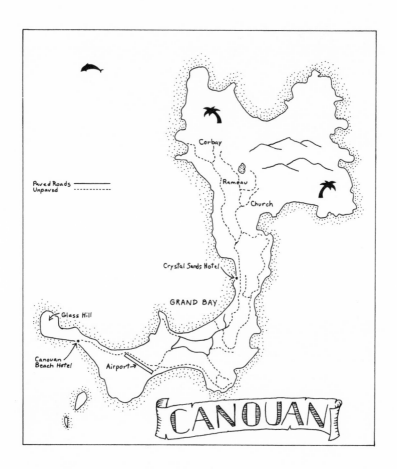

start at $50 single and $80 double, including breakfast and dinner.

CANOUAN BEACH HOTEL
P.O. Box 530
Canouan, St. Vincent, Grenadines
Telephone: (809) 45-844-13
This is the hotel that old-time visitors to Canouan felt was inevitable and that one day would spoil this tranquil island. Built on the other

side of the island from Crystal Sands, the new hotel is so inconspicuous that a visitor could sail by and miss it entirely. It is French-owned and the international clientele enjoy a wide variety of water sports, snorkeling and swimming off magnificent, uncrowded beaches. Rates start at $64 single and $128 double.

For visitors on a limited budget, *LE BIJOU GUEST HOUSE* has six basic rooms on the beach. Breakfast and dinner are included in the $25 single and $50 double rates.

FAVORITE SPOTS
On the island's east side there are many excellent, deserted beaches and coves which are easy to reach in less than an hour by foot. A deserted old church is all that remains of a village swept away by a hurricane in 1921.

WEATHER
Canouan gets less rain than other Grenadine islands—good for the visitor seeking sunshine, but necessary to remember when in the shower. Lack of abundant water will safeguard Canouan from over-development and keep the island uncrowded for many years. The few visitors who do arrive bring contact with the outside world, and new jobs for the young who would otherwise leave the island.

HOW TO GET THERE
Boat service from St. Vincent leaves on Monday and Thursday around 9 a.m. and arrives on Canouan in the afternoon. The boat returns on Tuesday and Friday. Air Martinique has flights from St. Vincent.

VENEZUELA

ISLA DE COCHE

Within view of the overdeveloped, heavily touristed Venezuelan resort destination of Isla Margarita lies a remarkable opportunity to literally "get away from it all." Just a 90-minute ferry boat ride or a 20 minute airplane flight from the frantic commercial bustle of Isla Margarita, Isla de Coche offers little more than a supremely tranquil setting for stress-free relaxation at shockingly affordable prices. The relatively flat and arid island is home to a thousand or so residents who depend upon fishing or intermittent salt manufacturing operations for their living. Tourist development is virtually non-existent—no T-shirts or souvenirs—and it is primarily vacationers from Caracas who cross over from Margarita to check out the absolute peace and quiet of this hidden oasis. But for the adventurous traveler who is looking only for a restful setting to enjoy the sea, the sun and delicious native cooking, Coche is a rugged chunk of paradise.

Our first sighting of Isla de Coche from the large passenger ferry that cruises over from Punta de Piedras on Margarita was ambiguous. From this northerly approach, the island appears to be mostly deserted, with a few strange buildings materializing into view. Drawing closer, we saw a string of houses near the long beach to the left of the ferry landing. They are part of a failed housing development near the salt extraction facilities. A huge, concrete, institutional-looking structure on the hill turns out to be the largest of the island's many churches. Far to the right, on the western tip of the island, a lonely stand of palm trees marks the foreigner's likely destination, Coche's only accommodation, the Hotel Turistico.

Initially, the island has a strangely desolate feeling. One or two taxis are waiting at the dock to take passengers on the short trip into San Pedro de Coche, the island's main village. The ride winds through dusty streets, past ramshackle buildings and cinder block housing in various states of construction and disrepair. But once settled into the hotel, with a cool drink and a friendly welcome from the young staff, the foreboding feeling of landing in an alien environment, where few tourists tread, melts into welcome sighs of relaxation. Upon arrival at the hotel, when our limited traveler's repertoire of Spanish was failing us, a visiting airline pilot set aside his coffee and tried to interpret with his limited English. Before long, several guests had joined in. Within a few hours we had made new acquaintances and discovered ways to communicate relatively clearly with our hosts (who turned out to speak plenty of English).

Coche's main appeal is the chance to escape from civilization into a culture that is virtually oblivious to the hyperactivity of mainland life. Add to that the warm and accommodating nature of the hotel staff and the other guests (almost all Venezuelan), and what seemed alien becomes comfortable and familiar. The daily life of Coche—the repair of fishing nets and boats, the early morning launches, the preparation of the catch, the late afternoon games in the streets or on the beaches—goes on undisturbed by the trickle of visitors.

Our first walk through the pueblo of San Pedro drew silent stares from curious children and bemused adults who rarely see North Americans on their streets. We felt like we had landed from another planet. After exploring the quiet streets of San Pedro, we decided to find a way to investigate the rest of the island. For about 100 *bolivars* an hour (less than $3), a driver will take you around the entire island: through the smaller villages of Guinima, Guamache and El Bichar; out past the airport and the salt processing sheds; along the vast white beach at Punta La Playa. If you are lucky, you will hear stories about

how the islanders drove a Catholic priest off Coche because he offended their traditional sensibilities. Taking us back to the 5 a.m. ferry on the morning of our departure, our driver, Bertrand, related how he had been visited by spirits in the night, both on the road to Guinima and in his own home. They took the form of nuns and young girls, he said, except for one old woman spirit who is known as "the quiet one."

Our finest hours on Coche were spent swimming in the calm Caribbean waters in the early morning before the considerable heat of noon, or at dusk, when the air was like velvet and large sea birds slanted against the crimson and orange cloud-dappled sky. At night, an unbelievable calm descended with the darkness, even as the evening breezes lifted and rattled the few palms. Sleep comes easily with the gentle rhythms of the waves upon the shore. All the cares you left behind melt away as Coche reminds you how to lose yourself in the long, peaceful moment.

FAVORITE SPOT

PUNTA LA PLAYA is the location of Coche's finest beach, a long arc of white sand around a cove of warm, shallow water. Other than the small beach at the hotel, this is the easiest place to swim. While you can have immense sections of beach all to yourself, be sure to either bring your own shade, for the *playa* is treeless, or avoid the hot midday hours. Other rockier spots on Coche's shore are excellent for shell collecting.

NOTEWORTHY

The *PANADERIA*, two blocks away from the hotel, is a large, relatively modern market providing fresh breads, cold drinks, bottled water and various canned and dry goods.

LOCAL FISHERMEN make their boats available for hire. They can take you to the nearby island of Cubagua or to various locations for fishing and snorkeling. Remember, there are no regular tourist services, such as dive shops, on Coche, so it is up to you to find local residents who can help you shape your own vacation. The Hotel Turistico staff knows many such islanders.

WHERE TO STAY

HOTEL TURISTICO
San Pedro de Coche
Isla Coche, Venezuela
Telephone: (095) 9-9177
Once you have arrived on Isla Coche, just ask your taxi driver to take you to "the hotel." Located on the western end of the island, at the northwestern corner of the main village of San Pedro, the Hotel Turistico is the only game in town. But this adequately maintained 16-room hotel does not exploit its unique position with high rates and careless service. Subsidized by the Venezuelan government, the hotel is operated by two young men, Miguel and Jesus, who look after the guests with charming enthusiasm. The rooms are right on the beach, with direct views of the beautiful Caribbean sunsets. While the accommodations are relatively spartan—whitewashed walls, red tile floors, ceiling fans, minimal furniture and cold water only in the bathrooms—they are clean and very reasonably priced. In the octagonal bar, the walls are decorated with felt marker graffiti and signatures of the hotel's guests, and loud Caribbean and American pop music often blares out of the stereo. The adjoining octagonal dining room looks out on the beach and the island's only stand of palm trees. Once you have settled into the slow, carefree rhythms of life on Coche, the Hotel quickly becomes a relaxing home, and the

guests and employees begin to feel like family. Rates are about $8 a night for a single, just under $10 for a double.

RESTAURANTS

Although San Pedro de Coche does have a few tiny bars and markets, the only place for travelers to eat is at the Hotel Turistico. The food is excellent. Local women prepare delicious soups with fresh fish, shrimp and crabs; *arepas* (a fried dough that is sometimes slightly sweet), rice and black beans, fried bananas, and a variety of fish and chicken dishes. The best dinners feature tomato and cheese salads, *tostones* (fried plantain), and *pargo*, a local fish related to grouper and snapper, grilled with garlic. Miguel and Jesus run a full bar, assisted by Orfeo, who speaks excellent English. One night they surprised us by cutting up a fresh cantaloupe and mixing it with crushed ice in a blender for a delicious and refreshing fruit drink. Two people can eat well and drink for less than $10 a day.

HOW TO GET THERE

Avensa Air and Linea Aeropostal Venezolana operate scheduled flights from Caracas (Maiquetia Airport) to Isla Margarita. The ferry to Coche departs from Punta de Piedras Monday through Thursday at 12:30 p.m., on Friday and Saturday at 10:30 a.m., and on Sundays at 8 a.m., 1:30 p.m., and 5:30 p.m. But, note that schedules can change and be sure to inquire, preferably in Spanish, at the terminal about the current times. The fare is about 50 cents.

Aero Taxi El Sol de America runs flights from Margarita to Coche twice daily, at 8 a.m. and 4:30 p.m., for about $6 per person. But check ahead of time because the service is not always in operation.

ISLA DE CUBAGUA

To the east of Isla de Coche lies the smaller island of Isla de Cubagua. The site of the first Spanish city in Venezuela, and once the site
of rich pearl fisheries, Cubagua is now a barren and windswept desert
island. On Coche, you can hear stories of how the Spaniards mer-
cilessly enslaved and murdered the original Indian population, and
how that original city was swept away centuries ago by a monstrous
storm. On Cubagua, you can walk through the rubble of stone that
makes up the "ruins" of the early settlement. The only signs of life
today are a few shacks used by local fishermen and a small marine
laboratory on one of the bays. The island itself is flat and scrubby,
its vegetation dominated by several varieties of blooming cactus.

The only way to get to Cubagua is to hire a fishing boat on Coche.
Felipe, who lives across the street from the Panaderia, will take you
in his partially covered inboard-engine boat for between $15 and $20.
You need to leave early in the morning so that you can return before
the sea gets rough in the afternoon. The ride takes about 1¼ hours.
Two or three hours are enough to explore the ruins, beachcomb, and
swim and snorkel around the reefs. The wreck of an old ferry marks
the entrance to Ensenada de Charagato. Large grey pelicans roost
on the rusted hull. In the quiet bay, sailboats anchor for shelter. It
is a fine spot for swimming and shelling, with a smooth sandy beach.
On shore, fishermen offered to sell us fresh lobster, but we opted for
a shell with a small pearl developing on its inner wall. A truly adventurous soul could probably camp for the night on Cubagua, but a

day trip is enough for a glimpse of a place where the distant past and the present are not very far apart.

NOTES

IMMIGRATION: A passport, but not a visa, is required for entrance into Venezuela.

CURRENCY: The Venezuelan currency is based on the Bolivar (B's). When the exchange rate is favorable to the dollar as it was in 1987, at about 31 B's to the dollar prices are outrageously low: coffee for about 3 cents, soft drinks for about 12 cents. On the way to Coche, the best place to exchange currency is right in the Maiquetia Airport.

If your schedule requires that you spend time on Isla Margarita, take best advantage of your time by enjoying one of the excellent restaurants in Porlamar—such as O Sole Mio Restaurant da Rosetta at Calle Cedeno y Calle Malave, or Restaurant Martin Pescador—that serve enormous portions of delicious lobster, in elegant settings, at bargain prices.

Although listed in some guidebooks as an uninhabited guano island, *ISLA LOS ROQUES*, in the Caribbean about 75 miles north of Caracas, was consistently recommended by native Venezuelans for its beautiful clear waters and gorgeous beaches. It supports a small fishing village, is accessible by small plane, and remains essentially undiscovered by most non-Venezuelans: a truly secluded hideaway for the adventurous traveler.

BELIZE

The cayes of Belize are the most hospitable and accessible of all the islands along the coast of Central America. Formerly British Honduras, and now a member of the British Commonwealth as an independent democratic nation, Belize is unique among Central American countries. It is an uncrowded country of only fifteen inhabitants per square mile. When the non-profit Freedom House Foundation ranked countries according to their respect for human rights and civil liberties, it grouped Belize with Britain, Canada and the United States. It is a safe and stable country with a literacy rate over 90%. The friendly and hospitable English-speaking inhabitants welcome visitors warmly, and are striving to develop a tourist industry to boost their declining sugar-based economy.

There are 175 islands off the coast of Belize! These beautiful cayes (pronounced "keys") are flat, narrow, beach-lined islands that are mostly populated by an incredible variety of birds. Less than a dozen cayes have any human inhabitants, and aside from several privately-owned resort islands and various research stations, only three cayes offer the visitor overnight accommodations. No other island group in the Caribbean has a larger or more spectacular barrier reef than Belize's, which is second in size only to the Great Barrier Reef of Australia.

Ambergris Caye, sharing a border with Mexico's Yucatan, is the most developed, yet remains quiet and off-the-beaten-track. Just south is Caye Caulker (pronounced and sometimes spelled "Caye Corker"). This island is even more secluded, a veritable bargain paradise where one can stay for as little as $4 a night or "splurge" on a hearty lobster dinner for $3.50! St. George's Caye is home to a few residents, one 12-room hand-built lodge and four thatch-roof cottages. The largest number of guests ever on the island at one time was 28. There are several lodges on private cayes: Turneffe Island Lodge on Caye Bokel; Lomont's on North East, Little and Long Cayes; Pyramid Island Resort on Caye Chapel; and the Wave Reef Resort on Gallows Point

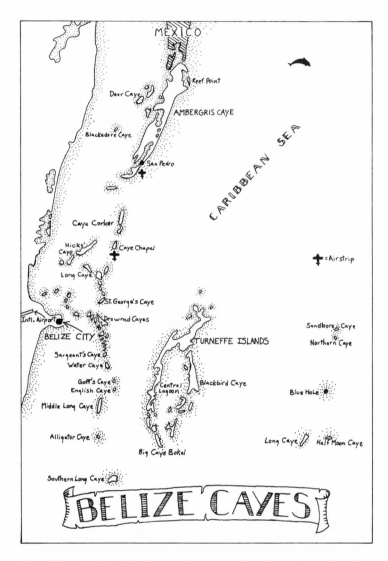

BELIZE CAYES

Caye. These isolated lodges are known only to the most avid scuba divers and fishermen who have discovered these waters to be among the world's finest diving and fishing destinations.

AMBERGRIS CAYE

The small, comfortable hotels that have opened in the last decade on Ambergris have not spoiled the sleepy atmosphere of this 35-mile long island. There may now be an air-conditioned luxury hotel or two, but the streets—"Front", "Middle", and "Back"—remain nothing more than hard-packed white sand. Automobiles are still rare.

San Pedro is the only town, with a white, dusty frontier look. The wooden buildings are parched and weathered by the salt and searing sun. Fishing still remains the island's chief concern, but tourism has brought employment and income to many who otherwise would have left the island. After a bountiful catch, picturesque fishing boats line the waterfront of San Pedro town. Fresh fish grilled to perfection is one of the pleasures of an Amergris stay.

Here on Ambergris, the reef is less than a mile offshore and the waves can be seen breaking easily along it. The pristine and virgin quality of the reef make it one of the world's best diving locations. Massive coral canyons, with depths of 50 to 100 feet, can be explored along the main barrier reef. Each canyon is full of caves and tunnels teeming with life, and it is not unusual to see a school of porpoises or huge turtles swimming along beside you.

For the novice snorkeler or swimmer, the area inside the reef is rarely deeper than 40 feet. Calm and protected, the water is a wonderland of brilliantly colored fish of fluorescent orange and purple, dazzling red and green, and electric blue. Above this boundless aquarium,

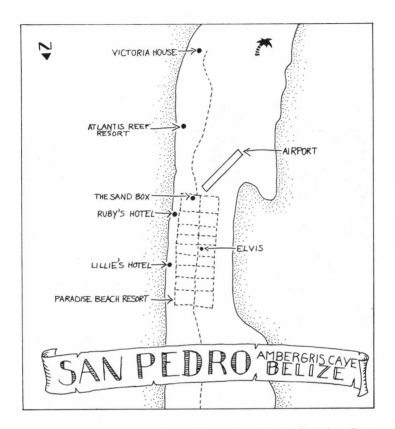

constant breezes provide ideal conditions for sailing and wind-surfing.

Time moves slowly on Ambergris. Dogs sleep at high noon on the sandy main street. Towards evening they amble aside for the San Pedro youngsters who play softball. Fishing, swimming, snorkeling, scuba diving, sailing, eating, reading, sleeping—there is much to be said for this lazy and rejuvenating way of life on Ambergris.

FAVORITE SPOT
HOL CHAN MARINE RESERVE, a four-and-one-half square mile

area at the south end of the Caye, opened as a National Park in May, 1987. This spectacular area has been set aside for the protection and observation of marine life and will become a major spawning area for hundreds of fish species.

WHERE TO STAY
PARADISE HOTEL
P.O. Box 888, Belize City
Telephone: (713) 850-1664
The Paradise is the nicest hotel right in town. Thatch-roofed cottages are arranged around a beachfront garden with bar and lounge areas. Rates start at $55 single and $75 double. Excellent food.

RUBIE'S HOTEL
San Pedro, Ambergris Caye, Belize

This budget hotel has no air-conditioning and no frills, but it is right on the beach, with good ventilation, and superb views in two directions. Rates are $20 with private bath and $15 without.

LILLY'S HOTEL
San Pedro, Ambergris Caye, Belize
Lilly's is similar to Rubie's, but some rooms have no views. Access is from the beach or through the backyards of adjoining buildings. There is a restaurant where meals can be had by advance arrangement. Rates are $10 per night without bath or view, and $12.50 per person with bath and view.

ATLANTIS REEF RESORT
San Pedro, Ambergris Caye, Belize
A short walk from town, this hotel offers thatch-roof cottages arranged around a beachfront courtyard. Rates are $35 single and $45 double.

HOUSEKEEPING APARTMENTS

HOUSE OF THE RISING SUN
San Pedro, Ambergris Caye, Belize
These new studios, with full kitchens and ceiling fans, are located on the beach a short distance from San Pedro.

Belize Promotions in Houston, owned by Tommy and Jerisue Thompson, can reserve and arrange economical air-hotel packages to Rising Sun and all other major accommodations in Belize. Telephone: (800) 231-0629, wait for a second dial tone, then dial 537.

RESTAURANTS
ELVIS, a sand-floored hut on the center street of town, features inexpensive local seafood with conch and lobster specialties.

SAND BOX is a good Mexican restaurant across the road from the airport in San Pedro town.

THE HUT, a moderately-priced popular restaurant, is noted for its turtle curry. Owner Shelley Prevett provides hard-to-get information (about babysitters, air charters, local black-coral jewelry-makers). Shelley's brother, Penny Arceo, is a knowledgeable instructor of bonefishing, snorkeling, diving and birdwatching.

HOW TO GET THERE

Tan Sahsa Airlines operates non-stop service from Miami (two hours), New Orleans and Houston. Challenge International and TACA International Airlines also serve Belize City. Allow time in Belize City to switch airports if you intend to fly on Maya or Tropic Air directly to San Pedro (a 20-minute flight that concludes with a landing on the bandaid sized airstrip). It is quite feasible to drive to Belize City from any point in the United States, then leave the car behind for the ferry trip to Ambergris, Caye Caulker or St. George Caye. A valid passport is required for entry to the country.

CAYE CAULKER

A few miles south of Ambergris is less visited and less expensive Caye Caulker. The island is so narrow that you can see the water on the other side as you approach one of the little docks which the locals call "bridges." The cay is virtually all beach, and the inhabited portion is so small that one can easily walk its length and breadth within an hour. It is a barefoot island: all the roads and paths are sand, free of rocks and broken glass. After a day or two, one gets to know many of the 450 friendly islanders and the visitors who come from all parts of the world. Local artist Phillip Lewis, whose work decorates the face of Belizean currency, sells his own map of the island which includes everything from where to get a massage to the entrance of the world's largest underwater cave system. Phillip knows everyone and greets visitors as he makes his daily stroll around the island. The friendliness and low prices of Caye Caulker tempt the visitor into long stays.

FAVORITE SPOTS
ELLEN MACRAE'S ART GALLERY: Ellen MacRae is not only a fine graphic artist, but is also a marine biologist who lectures on reef ecology and birdwatching. If the conditions are right, she will follow her lecture with a guided trip to the reef.

THE CUT: This deep channel slices through the island and is an ideal place for swimming, especially since much of the water around the island is so shallow. It is a local favorite for children, who enjoy the high diving from the branch of an overhanging tree.

WHERE TO STAY
THE ANCHORAGE
Caye Caulker, Belize

For the unbelievable rate of $5 per night per person, the Anchorage offers a charming stucco and thatch-roof cottage (with private bath, shower and hot water) on one of the prettiest beachfronts on the island. Joanne and Sam, expatriots from Alaska and Hawaii, welcome guests into their kitchen where there is a "coffee kitty" with a suggested donation of 25 cents. Joanne will also make to order coconut cream pastries and oatmeal cookies.

RIVA'S GUEST HOUSE

Above the Aberdeen Chinese Restaurant (which serves good food), are six rooms which rent for as little as $3.25 a night. The rooms are

small, spartan and without private facilities, but the view from the front porch is as fine as any on the island. You can watch the island population walk by in the evening as you sip a cool drink on the porch, with the colors of the sunset reflected on the blue Caribbean.

TROPICAL PARADISE HOTEL AND BEACH COTTAGES
Caye Caulker, Belize
This is the most expensive place to stay on the island, close to restaurants, but not as secluded or quiet as the Anchorage. Rates start at $9 per night and "soar" to $12.50!

RESTAURANTS
MARIN'S: The delicious lobster, served indoors or out in the garden, is as good as any outside of Maine. Two large tails with hot butter cost only $3.50. They were so tasty that even though I went back three times, I could never bring myself to try anything else!

TROPICAL PARADISE HOTEL RESTAURANT: This is the place to go for breakfast or lunch. You eat in the sunny courtyard, or inside where ceiling fans keep it pleasantly cool. My favorites are their conch fritters, which cost only 25 cents for a plate of two and are the size of hamburgers but much more satisfying.

WENDY'S: Wendy serves breakfast in her tiny cottage. Crepes with fresh fruit and homemade yogurt, including coffee, cost $1.50.

HOW TO GET THERE
For the time being, there is no airfield on Caulker. Morning boats from Belize City make the journey in about an hour-and-a- half. At Mom's Triangle Inn (a famous rendezvous spot), tour and boat information is posted on a bulletin board. Chocolat, who runs a boat

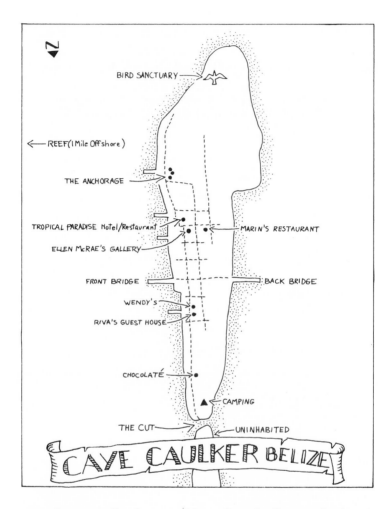

N

BIRD SANCTUARY

←— REEF(1 Mile Offshore)

THE ANCHORAGE

TROPICAL PARADISE Hotel/Restaurant

ELLEN McRAE'S GALLERY

MARIN'S RESTAURANT

FRONT BRIDGE

BACK BRIDGE

WENDY'S

RIVA'S GUEST HOUSE

CHOCOLATÉ

CAMPING

THE CUT

UNINHABITED

CAYE CAULKER BELIZE

every day except Sunday to and from Caye Caulker, can be found eating breakfast there every morning. He charges about $6 for one-way passage on the Soledad, his open boat which bounces like a roller-coaster as it speeds over the waves. Mangrove Islets appear through the salty spray as the mainland vanishes from view. Coming from nearby Ambergris, you can charter a boat for the short trip.

ST. GEORGE'S CAYE

Less than nine miles from Belize City Harbor, St. George's Caye was the first capital of British Honduras, from 1650 to 1784. It is reputed to be the scene of a great sea battle against the Spaniards in 1798. With only a small resident population, the island is much quieter today, and only a few reminders of its past endure. A sandy footpath parallels the coastline from the public pier. The swimming and snorkeling are excellent from any of the seven piers, or "bridges." Most of the spectacular dive sites are only ten to fifteen minutes from the dock of the island's only lodge.

WHERE TO STAY
ST. GEORGE'S LODGE
P.O. Box 625
Belize City, Belize
or
Belize Promotions
720 Worthshire
Houston, TX
Telephone: (713) 869-3614 or (800) 231-0629 ext. 537
The only accommodation on the island is St. George's Lodge, a secluded retreat handcrafted of local hardwoods. The beamed cathedral ceiling and handmade furniture in the public area are unique. The

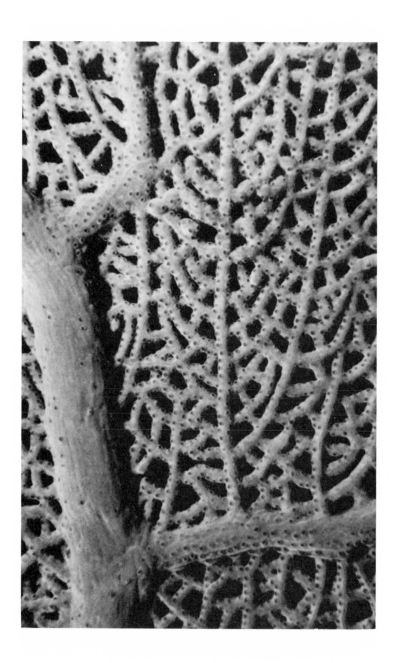

lodge has 12 rooms in the main building and four thatch-roof cottages built over the ocean. Expensive.

HOW TO GET THERE

Occasional boats from Belize City make the 20 minute crossing to the public pier, but most visitors are guests at the Lodge and are met by private boat.

Outside Belize's barrier reef are three spectacular atolls (ring-shaped coral islands surrounding a lagoon). Rarely found outside the South Pacific, the three in Belizean waters—Lighthouse Reef, Turneffe Reef and Glover's Reef—are a nature lover's dream. They are far removed from civilization, surrounded by an azure sea teeming with rare and exotic marine life.

GLOVER'S REEF: LONG CAYE, LITTLE CAYE AND NORTH EAST CAYE

Long Caye, located on the edge of a 2000 foot drop-off, is 2000 feet long and 500 feet wide, formed of coral and white sand piled up as high as ten feet on the reef. According to the earliest maps, it was already well-planted with coconut tress in 1700. Ten rustic rental cabins that have been built on the beach overlooking the coral reef are well-suited to the adventurous ocean and sun lover seeking a remote, quiet spot far from the noise of city life.

Little Caye, just to the north of Long Caye, is the smallest undiscovered island mentioned in this book: a one-half acre private retreat covered with palm trees. It is rare anywhere in the Caribbean to have the opportunity to live in a cottage on one's own private island, but the Lomont family can provide exactly that experience. Their two-bedroom cabin, with upstairs kitchen, includes a free dug-out canoe in the $50 daily rate.

North East Caye, also owned by the Lomont Family, is the location of their Glover's Reef Village, a group of well-spaced rustic cottages, restaurant and bar. The Village caters to divers who enjoy exploring sites where "no one has dived before".

WHERE TO STAY
LOMONT'S GLOVER REEF VILLAGE & RENTAL CABINS
c/o Mrs. Beth LaCroix
P.O. Box 1158
Belize City, Belize
Telephone: (501) 2331

HOW TO GET THERE
Day trips are not recommended. In fact, they might be impossible as it is a seven-hour boat trip to Glover's Reef from Belize City. The Lomont family arranges boat transportation for all guests.

TURNEFFE REEF: CAYE BOKEL

Caye Bokel is 12.4 acres of sand beach and coconut palms. Turneffe Diving Lodge has long operated here as a very small, first-rate fishing camp. Scuba diving is now included, as there is excellent diving within ten minutes of the island's dock. Sites include the wreck of the Sayonara, the Majestic Reef (with black coral trees in 50 feet of water), the Elbow, and Half-Moon Caye. The Lodge's boat meets guests in Belize City.

NOTEWORTHY
LIGHTHOUSE REEF
Less than two hours by boat from Caye Bokel, the Lighthouse Reef is an uninhabited chain visited only by the most adventurous divers. The Blue Hole, the mysterious underwater shaft explored by Jacques Cousteau, is more than 400 feet deep and features magnificent stalactite formations.

WEATHER
The weather is sunny and warm throughout the year, with almost constant trade winds blowing. Two or three times during the winter months, a north storm brings rain and cold wind for three to five days. Hurricanes are uncommon, but if they do occur, it will likely be in August or September.

NOTES

Mosquitoes and small insects might be a problem at certain times of the year. Jungle Juice, Cutter's, or Avon Bath Oil are good deterrents. Most insects cannot fly when there is a breeze, so a fan can be useful at night.

Although primitive in some ways, Belize is both healthy and safe. Water is drinkable almost everywhere, and inoculations are not needed. For a poor country, there is a remarkable lack of both theft and panhandling. The people are friendly, helpful, and proud.

If time allows, visits to the Mayan sites of Xunantunich and Altun Ha, on the mainland, are richly rewarding. Belize is a natural wonder, supporting over 500 species of exotic birds and 250 varieties of orchids, and it is one of the last habitats for the elusive jaguar.

WEST CARIBBEAN

ISLA MUJERES

Change comes slowly to Isla Mujeres. Although the "Island of the Women" is just a short boat ride away from the plastic glamor and programmed vacationland of Cancun, it resists the invasion of time-share condos and tennis courts. Isla Mujeres may be one of the least hidden of the Caribbean's hidden islands, as more and more North Americans and Europeans discover its charms, but it still exists as a world apart from the luxury hotels and designer luggage across the water.

The narrow, five-mile long island sustains an extraordinary balance of tourism and the authentic indigenous life of a Mexican fishing village. Although large parties of Cancunites cruise over on tour boats for day trips of snorkeling and buffets, they usually stay away from the town in their pre-planned outings. And while certain omens of modernization have crept in—satellite television dishes at a few bars, air conditioning in several hotels—there are small signs of deferred progress: small plane service from the Cancun airport to the Isla Mujeres army base airstrip seems to have been discontinued, and the boldest attempt at a high-rise luxury hotel is already looking a bit weather-beaten in its isolated location at the northern tip of the island. New construction proceeds very slowly and it is visually offset by the older, time-worn architecture and tempered by the leisurely pace of life determined by geography and climate. So Isla Mujeres is not overwhelmed by rampant growth and its attractions of gorgeous beaches, bountiful fishing, and, if Jacques Cousteau is to be taken at his word, some of the best snorkeling in the world, can all be enjoyed in a relatively serene atmosphere.

The island is accessible by ferry boats from two different mainland locations. From the fishing village of Puerto Juarez, five miles north of Cancun, a passenger ferry leaves for Isla Mujeres about every two hours throughout the day. Three miles further north, at Punta Sam, an auto ferry (which also carries passengers without vehicles), makes the trip on a slightly less frequent basis. Although you can drive around the island, there are few places to go of any considerable distance, and transportation is cheap and abundant—taxi fares are regulated and small motor bikes are available by the hour or the day. So there is no compelling reason to make the trip with an automobile.

At Puerto Juarez, a small information booth is located at the wharf, where you can obtain information about the next departure. You might be offered passage on a private boat, but the fare is likely to be seven or eight times the cost of the ferry. On the dock, vendors sell succulent fruits from pushcarts, including apples and mangos peeled and carved into the shapes of flowers. Along the shoreline, donkeys bray in nearby yards and exotic birds screech in the palms.

Like an oversized version of the African Queen, the large wooden boat chugs in across the calm waters and ties up to the dock. For a half-hour or so, passengers climb on board and settle onto the wooden benches. On one trip you are likely to hear four or five different languages, including perhaps French, German and Swedish, as well as Spanish and English, reflecting the diversity of mostly youthful tourists mixing with local commuters. Young Mexican men and women load on large bundles of locally produced hammocks, pinatas and other handicrafts, for sale on the island. Already, as the boat sets off on its 45-minute voyage across the sea, the slightly crazed rush of arriving in Cancun and hustling to Puerto Juarez has subsided, melting into the soothing warm and salty breeze.

Isla Mujeres was named by Spanish explorers in 1517. Impressed

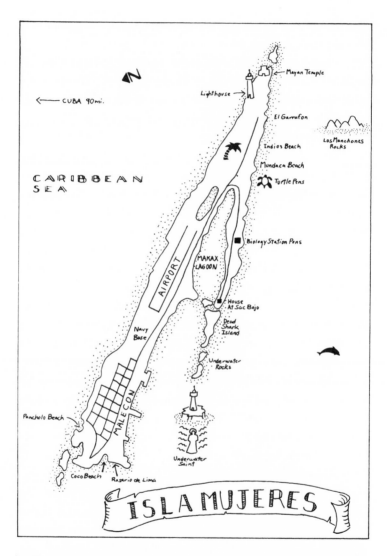

by the many female icons they found on the island, the conquistadors called it "Island of Women." Today, the last remaining vestige of the original Mayan civilization is a small temple ruin at the rocky southernmost tip. As you approach the island by ferry, however, the evidence of modernism gathers shape on the northwestern shore, where the hotels, restaurants and tourist shops are crowded together amidst the houses and shops of the island population. Tall palm trees rise up around the densely constructed town, enhancing the exotic image of the island, which is otherwise fairly flat and covered mostly by scrubby jungle.

At the landing, the commotion of tourists, taxis, and vendors can be initially intimidating. The taxi stand is located next to the dock, but almost all the restaurants and hotels are within walking distance. During the tourist season, it is wise to make reservations in advance. Otherwise, Isla Mujeres offers a full range of accommodations. Several medium-priced hotels, such as the Vistal Mar, to more expensive modern hotels, like the Posada del Mar, are located along the Avenida Rueda Medina, which runs from the pier along the western beach-front. Towards the northern tip of the island, near the snow white sands of Playa Los Cocos, are the inexpensive concrete and thatched-roof bungalows of the Cabanas Zazil-Ha, while further around the island's tip, past Playa Norte, stands the beautifully located but preten-tiously designed and surprisingly non-luxurious 100-room Hotel El Presidente Caribe. Two resort hotels are situated out of town, down the western coast: Maria's, with romantic pink stucco bungalows around a shady palm garden, and a French restaurant with outdoor dining; and Hacienda Gomar, an ambitious complex with shops, hotel rooms, and a large dining room and terrace near the beach.

For the least expensive, centrally located hotels, follow one of the narrow streets (Aves. Morelos and Bravo) straight ahead from the pier. In the interior of town you'll find a variety of small, inexpensive and moderately priced hotels—the Hotels Martinez, Berny, Osorio, Cara-col, and Caribe Maya, for instance—some with air conditioning, others with only ceiling fans. On the eastern rocky side of the island, only a three block walk, two hotels overlook the rough surf of the ocean: the newer Rocas del Caribe, and the slightly older, more picturesque Hotel Rocamar, perched on a high corner of town right above the town square.

Once settled, you can start your explorations of the island. The town, just a few blocks wide and only slightly longer, readily becomes familiar. Street names are of little use, but it's virtually impossible to get lost, as you quickly learn such major reference points as the pier, the zocalo (town square), the lighthouse tower, and the hotels and restaurants. You also begin to recognize the faces around town. The people are smiling and friendly, and yet go about their business without undue attention to the tourists. Fellow visitors become neighbors and share stories over dinner. You become aware of the changes in the light—hard and bright under blue skies, or soft and muted under the cloud cover of a passing tropical storm. And you become conscious of the pervasive, intoxicating scent of mangos and papayas in the air. Within a day, the warm city and the sultry weather fit comfortably, like a well-worn shirt.

The Avenida Hidalgo is the main central street, running north from the town square. It's been modestly reshaped and landscaped into a narrow mall and, like most of the streets, is well lighted at night. A stroll down Avenida Hidalgo and out along the branching byways is enough for you to get your bearings.

The town offers a great temptation to laze around in the sun on the beaches, browse leisurely through the many shops, stop for a snack and a beer at one of the many *taquerias* and restaurants, or just sit and watch children playing baseball or futbol (soccer) on the beach. At Playa Norte, the best place to swim at the edge of town, young athletic travelers play volleyball and stretch out on the sand, taking breaks at the two snack bars on the beach. The streets of the village bustle with activity until siesta, when many businesses shut down for the afternoon rest. At dusk, the town jumps back to life. A heated basketball game, on the Jose Del C. Pastrana court in the zocala,

usually starts up at sundown, with local teens and young adults teaming against the tourists. Fans gather spontaneously and cheer one side or the other, taking breaks to fetch a fresh milk shake from the corner ice cream stand, or a cold drink from the supermarket across the square, next to the movie house.

As night falls, the town begins to shimmer with increased activity under the bright streetlights. People line up at the pushcarts in front of the supermarket to buy fresh fruit. Children play in the streets and in the broad plaza in front of the Teatro del Pueblo. A net is strung across the court, and volleyball replaces basketball as the sports attraction. Tourists, relaxed and contented from a hearty dinner, wander slowly through the shops. Occasionally, a band sets up its equipment and plays popular Caribbean music from the steps of the municipal building.

But the pleasures of Isla Mujeres extend far beyond the town. With the early rise of the tropical sun, a whole different landscape of adventures unfolds. Although it's not out of the question to walk, and while taxis are very cheap, the fun way to explore the island is on a motorbike, which can be rented from several locations for less than $10 a day. A short loop around the northern end takes you to Playa Los Cocos, the best swimming beach, and to the lagoon near the El Presidente. The two-lane road south along the western shoreline, the Garrafon Highway, leads past the small army base and the Makas Lagoon. The island's other main swimming beach, Playa Lancheros, is just off the road, with shady *palapa* shelters, a snack stand, and wooden pens for sea turtles.

Near Playa Lancheros is the decaying estate of the 19th century slave trader, Fermin Mundaca. The pirate built his fortress on Isla Mujeres in the mid-1800s, creating his own paradise of grand buildings and gardens. All that remain of his lush Hacienda de la Huerta, (Estate of the Happy Orchard), are shady yet evocative ruins.

Further south is the island's most wondrous natural resource, El

Garrafon. Here, the combination of a large coral reef and exceptionally clear, gentle water provides hours of dazzling snorkeling. The beach is set up as a park, with a nominal entry fee, and is geared for heavy tourist traffic. A restaurant, an aquarium/museum, hamburger and ice cream stands, shops with clothes, curios, and snorkel equipment rentals are scattered across the terraced hillside. Large numbers of tourists are boated in daily from Cancun, but the crowd thins out in the mid-afternoon, and the snorkeling is spectacular. Hundreds of species of fish, of every imaginable color and shape, blithely feed on the reef and swim by in enormous schools.

If you can bear to leave El Garrafon, the southern tip of the island is just a half-kilometer away. A path leads past the lighthouse to the small remains of a Mayan temple, dramatically perched on the cliff above the crashing waves. Most people return to town on the same highway, but the road loops around to the eastern coastline where the shore is rugged and beautiful. The deserted beaches, with their heavier surf and gusty breezes, provide a chance to be alone, away from all the others who are "getting away from it all," to comb the beach, gather shells and driftwood, and watch the waves.

Any appetite worked up during an adventurous day on Isla Mujeres can be easily satisfied. Taquerias and restaurants abound in every price range. Although what is conventionally considered "Mexican food" is available, and some of the enchiladas, tortas, and *chilaquiles* are quite good, the main fare of the island is grilled fresh fish, served with lime, rice, and fresh handmade tortillas. The smaller restaurants, such as Sergio's, the Buccanero, La Mano de Dios, or Giltry, are very inexpensive, with entire meals for two or three dollars. Such larger, fancier establishments as Gomar, Ciro's, or Maria's, specializing in lobster, shrimp, conch and turtle, are hardly bargains, but provide fine service and a hint of luxury. For breakfast, the ideal setting can be found at the outdoor restaurants on the beach near the pier, where you can sit under thatched roofs and watch the boats go out.

If somehow the island grows too small, many planned excursions are available through hotels, stores, restaurants, or stands near the pier. The most popular day trip is to Isla Contoy, an uninhabited island north of Isla Mujeres, with a National Park bird sanctuary. Several entrepreneurs organize an entire day's outing that includes fishing, grilling and eating the catch, and snorkeling, with a long stopover on Contoy to observe the stunning variety of cormorants, pelicans, herons, egrets and other birds. Scuba diving and deep sea fishing trips can also be easily arranged.

A day or two is obviously not enough in which to savor all the delights of Isla Mujeres. But the island's most attractive characteristic is the freedom it provides the visitor — to choose from a variety of activities and adventures, to shape your own days and nights, and to determine your own pace. Somewhere between the overdevelopment of nearby Cancun and the natural state of a desert island, Isla Mujeres waits, a crossroads temporarily suspended in time, with almost any direction possible.

WHERE TO STAY
Consistent with its gradual development as a tourist spot, Isla Mujeres features all kinds of accommodations, from the upscale tackiness of the towering El Presidente, which dominates a prime location on the northwest tip of the island, to a few relatively remote establishments on the western coast, and dozens of small, modest hotels scattered around town. Among the latter are the Isleno, the Caracol, the Caribe Maya and the Osorio, all costing between about $15 and $20 a night for a double room.

HOTEL ROCAMAR
Ave. Nicolas Bravoy
Isla Mujeres, Quintana Roo, Mexico

Telephone: 988-2-01-01
Located on the eastern side of the island, at the corner of the town square, the Hotel Rocamar sits right on the edge of the sea. Most of the large rooms have balconies perched virtually on top of the breakers. Although there are signs of weathering and minor disrepair, the Rocamar boasts a certain charm and is one of the island's best deals. The combination of ceiling fans and constant sea breeze keeps the rooms cool, and the roaring song of the surf lulls you to sleep at night. Rates start at about $15 double.

POSADA DEL MAR
Avenida Rueda Marina No.15
Isla Mujeres, Quintano Roo, Mexico
Telephone: 992-6-04-22
Designed for the traveler who wants a bit of luxury without the completely plastic nature of the Cancun resorts (or Isla Mujeres' own highrise El Presidente), the Posada del Mar has 46 rooms and bungalows (with air-conditioning or ceiling fans) spread out around its neatly maintained palm gardens and grounds. Facing the western beach, it offers such amenities as a fountain-fed swimming pool, restaurant and patio bar. Rates start at about $36 double.

MARIA'S KANKIN
PO Box 69
77400 Isla Mujeres, Quintano Roo, Mexico
No Telephone
Perfect for a romantic getaway in the honeymoon spirit, Maria's Kankin is tucked into a lush setting of palms, mangos and flowering vegetation. Its pink stucco exterior adds to the charm of the terraced design. The patio bar and restaurant look out over the hotel's private beach.

RESTAURANTS

It would take more than a week to eat your way through Isla Mujeres, so numerous and diverse are the restaurants. Using your instinct, pocketbook and, best of all, tips from other travelers, you can make dining another branch of exploration.

SERGIO'S, on the east side of town, facing the town square, is an inexpensive spot for good fried fish. Its patio dining area is also a good spot to sit in the early evening for a cold drink and a snack of guacamole and chips.

THE BUCCANERO, an open air restaurant in the middle of town, serves excellent enchiladas, very cold soft drinks and beer, and a variety of local specialties.

MARIA'S KANKIN is romantically situated in a classically tropical setting out of town on the western coast of the island. The outdoor dining room is nestled in palms and looks out over the water. Menus are handprinted on woven straw mats. The dishes include local seafood excellently prepared in Mexican and continental styles. Although it is one of the more expensive places to eat on Isla Mujeres, it is also one of the loveliest.

EL LIMBO is a grotto-like restaurant nestled under the Hotel Rocamar. Its decor is simple but intriguing, with a seashell motif reflected in the tile floor and walls. Windows overlook the breakers on the eastern coast. The food is very good, with different varieties of fresh seafood prepared in several local styles. Watch out for the salsa: it is fiery.

BRISAS DEL CARIBE, a thatch-roofed patio restaurant located a few steps from the ferry dock, is a perfect place for a sunrise breakfast.

Fresh orange juice and delicious banana hotcakes are among the offerings.

CIRO'S LOBSTER HOUSE is one of the two or three large restaurants in the central section of the village. Although it is tourist oriented, with a fully stocked bar and a television set, many of the dishes are excellent. Lobster is the specialty, but the menu is extensive, and the soups are delicious.

NOTEWORTHY

SNORKELING, at El Garrafon: The coral reef, the remarkably clear waters and the abundance of exotic tropical fish conspire to provide some of the most accessible and intriguing snorkeling in the Caribbean. A nominal admission fee is required for entrance into the park. Equipment rentals are available at the beach. If the area around the main channel looks crowded, enter the water near the long pier to the left.

MOTORBIKING: Available for rent at several locations, the small motorscooters and mopeds are the best, if not cheapest, way to see the entire island. They are easy to drive, relatively safe, and can carry you to places you might not otherwise discover.

HOW TO GET THERE

From Cancun, travel by taxi or bus to Puerto Juarez and take the passenger ferry to Isla Mujeres. With an automobile, drive to Punta Sam, three miles north of Puerto Juarez, and take the car ferry.

ISLA HOLBOX

As you ride through the Yucatan jungle towards Chiquila, the mainland harbor nearest Isla Holbox, it's as if layers of civilization and pretense are peeled away before your eyes, preparing you for the simple fishing village island which rests an hour's boat ride across the sea. Along Highway 180, between Merida and Puerto Juarez, the tourists zoom back and forth, to Chichen Itza and Cancun, oblivious to the remote beauty to the north. But once you make the turn at the junction just west of Nuevo Xcan, the pace slackens and the quiet nature of the villages along the road takes hold.

Isla Holbox lies off the northeastern tip of the Yucatan peninsula, surrounded by the clear blue Gulf waters. Although it is 15 miles long and two miles across at its widest point, the island is inhabited only at the western end, where the small *pueblo* of Holbox, with perhaps a hundred houses, is located. Its people live by grace of the sea and their own small gardens. Since few tourists ever find their way to Isla Holbox, the island offers a tranquil picture of indigenous life where the Gulf of Mexico meets the Caribbean, unspoiled by the crass commerce of hotels, restaurants and curio shops. Without the lure of the typical resort town amenities and tourist attractions, Holbox challenges the visitor to creatively explore the unadorned setting and all its intrinsic beauty.

Much of the adventure is in getting there. Chiquila is within a few hours' drive of Cancun, Coba, or Valladolid, and public buses run on a regular schedule from highway 180, timed to meet the ferries to Isla Holbox. The paved two-lane road is good and the sparse traffic moves briskly between the towns on the 46 mile/75km stretch from El Ideal to Chiquila. But as each village crops up almost rhythmically along the way, and as the jungle flora gradually changes from the dense inland growth to the lighter vegetation nearing the seashore the scenery grows more absorbing and you find yourself slowing down to take it all in. Each small town has its variations on the same themes. Around the houses with their thatched *palapa* roofs, lines of bright-colored laundry sway in the breeze — reds, purples and yellows set off against the dark green tropical foliage. Chickens, hogs and turkeys amble along the roadside, sometimes crossing your path at their own leisure. Children stare intently as you drive by, their faces sometimes breaking into friendly smiles as they shyly respond to a wave. Every *pueblo* seems to have a baseball diamond and a basketball court, and such larger ones as Kantunilkin and San Angel, have *zocalos*, or town squares, surrounded by the few necessary businesses.

At the end of the road, Chiquila appears to be little more than a few houses and a solitary boat dock with only the slightest activity between the arrivals and departures of the ferries. There are no places to eat or stay in this tiny port, so you must time your arrival to the boat schedule. Even then, be open to unforeseen circumstances. On our first attempt to reach Holbox, we arrived at Chiquila in the afternoon during an especially blustery storm. The wind was creating large whitecaps on the sea, and blowing the warm heavy rain horizontally across the pier. When the ferries arrived from Holbox, the passengers were drenched. The captain of the auto ferry decided not to chance the return trip. We opted to drive back to Coba and return in the morning rather than brave the turbulent waves on the passenger ferry.

A large scow, able to transport two small cars or a truck, serves as the car ferry, but as there is virtually no driving to do on Holbox, you can leave your car near the dock and take the passenger boat, which can carry up to 50 people inside. The captain and his mate tie the boat to the pier and assist the passengers aboard, waiting to collect the fare during the hour-long trip. You ride with the regulars who commute to work or shop on the mainland, and are unlikely to encounter any English-speaking travelers.

The ride is slow, rolling, and as smooth as the weather will allow. If a storm whips up, bringing the sea to a froth, the boat rocks and dips like a roller coaster. But on a calm day, the trip is easy and comfortable. As Isla Holbox comes into view, you may notice a bold swatch of pink in a lagoon off to the left. As the boat draws closer, a sudden commotion erupts and the patch of bright pink starts to scatter and rise, as the large flock of flamingos takes flight. Launching their gangly bodies into graceful motion, the exotic birds soar in great circles and land in the shallow water once the boat has passed. It's just the first glimpse of Holbox's simple but elegant natural wonders.

Where the ferry docks, a dirt road leads from the pier into the village. If you arrive in mid-morning, with the sun already high in the sky, the *pueblo* may look parched and desolate. A baseball diamond sits in disrepair off to the right. Only a few people are visible on the dusty streets, and the disembarking passengers seem to vanish mysteriously on the trek into town. But the hidden life and appeal of Holbox gradually unfold as you leave the pier.

Just 50 yards or so from the dock stands the only restaurant, the El Paso—a screened, circular patio with a palm roof. The town is comprised of only five to ten square blocks of houses, and as you walk through, you will catch glimpses of women preparing meals and doing laundry, and children playing games in the small yards. Among the first things to catch your eye along the street are great piles of large conch and other shells near every house, discarded casually after the shellfish has been removed. Those shells indicate the main natural resource and livelihood of Holbox, and are the prime reward for the exploring traveler.

If you walk straight ahead on the road from the pier, you come quickly to the other side of the island where the fishing boats are tied up, and where a breathtaking expanse of white beach extends for a mile to the west and two miles to the east. Large pelicans and other seabirds amble along the shore or swoop overhead. Here, along the open sea, with its surprisingly gentle, clear blue waters, is the chief allure of Holbox for the adventurous visitor—a beachcomber's paradise. Just a few minutes' walk down the beach takes you away from the village, where there is nothing but shallow ocean to one side and the tangled scrub of jungle to the other.

The sand is littered with millions of shells of every variety. In some places they cover the beach completely, crunching under foot as you walk along. There is perhaps no greater abundance of whelks, cockles, bubbles, lion's paws and other shells anywhere else along the Yucatan peninsula. The first sight of all those treasures is overwhelming, and as you walk along the shore, the realization sinks in that they are just a tiny representation of the rich and varied life in the surrounding sea. And except for a fishing boat or two, you may come across no other signs of life. At many points along the deserted beach, you can wade out a great distance into the water and cool your feet or swim.

If you arrive at Holbox in the morning, you can get in two or three hours of relaxed beachcombing before walking back to the village. The activity picks up as families prepare for their midday meals, frying the day's catch, pounding corn meal into tortillas and cooking up pots of beans and rice. After several hours of beachcombing, we walked back through town and encountered the ferryboat skipper on his stopover between runs. He commented on the conch shells we had picked up, reminded us of the departure time and directed us to the restaurant, near the pier. At the El Paso, the fare is determined by what the sea has yielded to the fishermen that day. Generous, delicious portions of grilled fish are served with a stack of fresh, warm, home-made corn tortillas. Black beans are served in a flavorful broth, with sliced hot peppers on the side. Add a cold bottle of beer, soda or mineral water, and you could not ask for a heartier, more satisfying meal for the price (about $2).

Isla Holbox can be enjoyed for the day without much more than the few words of Spanish needed to order a meal and ask directions, but a fluent command of the language will allow you greater access to the life of the island. As there are no commercial accommodations on Holbox, if you want to stay for more than a day to explore more of the beach and to swim or fish, bring a sleeping bag or hammock and camp out down the beach, or be prepared to negotiate a housing rental with one of the islanders. Their shelter is extremely simple, with cement floors, wooden, tin or stucco walls, and minimal furnishings. If you plan to visit Holbox in one day, be sure to check the departure time of the ferry returning to Chiquila. However long you stay, the subtle magic of the remote island lingers well after you've watched the island slowly vanish behind you as the ferry takes you back to the Yucatan mainland.

HOW TO GET THERE

Take a car or bus to the village of Chiquila, 46 miles/75 km north from the 180 highway at El Ideal. The ferry leaves Chiquila for Isla Holbox three times a day, at 8 a.m., 11:30 a.m. and 3:30 p.m. (weather permitting) and makes the trip from Holbox at 6:30 a.m., 10 a.m. and 2:00 p.m.

EPILOGUE

Island enthusiasts take note: there are many more undiscovered islands not included in this book. Accustomed as I was to the expanses of the Pacific, Asia and Europe, I assumed the Caribbean was a relatively small and finite area. Instead, the more I traveled to over 100 islands the larger the Caribbean became. Each time I visited an island group I learned of a dozen more islands "just beyond." This was especially true in the seemingly endless chain of Family Islands in the Bahamas. Beyond Exuma and Long Island lie such hideaways as Farmer's Cay, Crooked Island, Acklins, the Jumento Cays (Ragged Island, Flamingo Cay, Nurse Cay), and Mayaguana Island—with a four-room Sheraton!

The adventurous traveler might also explore the hundreds of islands around the coast of Cuba, from the large Isla de Pinos to the many small cays of the Sabana Archipelago. Off Haitian shores, Ile de la Tortue, Ile de la Gonave, Isla Beata and Isla Saona await their first visitors.

The Caribbean stretches westward to the Central American coast as well, encompassing the Bay Islands off Honduras and the Corn Islands off Nicaragua, and far to the south where it shimmers along the beaches of Colombia's San Andres and Providencia islands. Panama's exotic San Blas islands are well worth visiting for their colorful matriarchal Indian culture and beautiful beaches.

Enchanted islands sometimes appear where you least expect them. During several visits to Marie-Galante and les Saintes in the French West Indies, I bypassed islands that guidebooks described as "flat, barren and uninhabited." But when I later ventured forth on my own, I was surprised to find a little jewel off Guadeloupe: an ancient South Atlantic mountain rising from the sea.

The Caribbean harbors many more such opportunities for discovery and exploration for the intrepid traveler willing to make the extra effort. The more challenging the journey, the greater the rewards of secluded destinations with undiscovered charms and hidden beauty.

PHOTO CREDITS

PUBLICATIONS

People's Guide to RV Camping in Mexico, Carl Franz $12.95 (91-5) 356 pp.

The sequel to *The People's Guide to Mexico,* this revised guide focuses on the special pleasures and challenges of RV travel in Mexico. An unprecedented number of Americans and Canadians have discovered the advantages of RV travel in reaching remote villages and camping comfortably on beaches. Sept '88

The On and Off the Road Cookbook, Carl Franz $8.50 (27-3) 272 pp.

Carl Franz, (*The People's Guide to Mexico)* and Lorena Havens offer a multitude of delicious alternatives to the usual campsite meals or roadside cheeseburgers. Over 120 proven recipes.

The Shopper's Guide to Mexico, Steve Rogers & Tina Rosa $9.95 (90-7) 200 pp.

The only comprehensive handbook for shopping in Mexico, this guide ferrets out little-known towns where the finest handicrafts are made and offers shopping techniques for judging quality, bargaining, and complete information on packaging, mailing and U.S. customs requirements. Sept '88

The Heart of Jerusalem, Arlynn Nellhaus $12.95 (79-6) 312 pp.

Denver Post journalist Arlynn Nellhaus draws on her vast experience in and knowledge of Jerusalem to give travelers a rare inside view and practical guide to the Golden City — from holy sites and religious observances to how to shop for toothpaste and use the telephone.

Guide to Buddhist Meditation Retreats, Don Morreale $12.95 (94-X) 312 pp.

The only comprehensive directory of Buddhist centers, this guide includes first-person narratives of individuals' retreat experiences. Invaluable for both newcomers and experienced practitioners who wish to expand their contacts within the American Buddhist Community. Sept. '88

Complete Guide to Bed & Breakfasts, Inns & Guesthouses, Pamela Lanier $13.95 (82-6) 520 pp.

Newly revised and the most complete directory, with over 4800 listings in all 50 states, 10 Canadian provinces, Puerto Rico and the U.S. Virgin Islands. This classic provides details on reservation services and indexes identifying inns noted for antiques, decor, conference facilities and gourmet food.

All-Suite Hotel Guide, Pamela Lanier $11.95 (70-2) 312 pp.

Pamela Lanier, author of *The Complete Guide to Bed & Breakfasts, Inns & Guesthouses,* now provides the discerning traveler with a listing of over 600 all-suite hotels. Indispensable for families traveling with children or business people requiring an extra meeting room.

Elegant Small Hotels, Pamela Lanier $13.95 (77-X) 202 pp.

This lodging guide for discriminating travelers describes 168 American hotels characterized by exquisite rooms and suites and personal service par excellence. Includes small hotels in 35 states and the Caribbean with many photos in full color.

Gypsying After 40, Bob Harris $12.95 (71-0) 312 pp.

Retirees Bob and Megan Harris offer a witty and informative guide to the "gypsying" lifestyle that has enriched their lives and can enrich yours. For 10 of the last 18 years they have traveled throughout the world living out of camper vans and boats. Their message is: "Anyone can do it'!!

Mona Winks, A Guide to Enjoying the Museum of Europe, Rick Steves $12.95 (85-0) 356 pp.

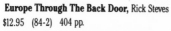

Here's a guide that will save you time, shoe leather and tired muscles. It's designed for people who want to get the most out of visiting the great museums of Europe. It covers 25 museums in London, Paris, Rome, Venice, Florence, Amsterdam, Munich, Madrid and Vienna.

Europe Through The Back Door, Rick Steves $12.95 (84-2) 404 pp.

Doubleday and Literary Guild Bookclub Selection.

For people who want to enjoy Europe more and spend less money doing it. In this revised edition, Rick shares more of his well-respected insights. He also describes his favorite "back doors" — less visited destinations throughout Europe that are a wonderful addition to any European vacation.

Europe 101, Rick Steves & Gene Openshaw $11.95 (78-8) 372 pp.

The first and only jaunty history and art book for travelers makes castles, palaces and museums come alive. Both Steves and Openshaw hold degrees in European history, but their real education has come from escorting first-time visitors throughout Europe.

Asia Through The Back Door, Rick Steves & John Gottberg $11.95 (58-3) 336 pp.

In this detailed guide book are information and advice you won't find elsewhere — including how to overcome culture shock, bargain in marketplaces, observe Buddhist temple etiquette and, possibly most important of all, how to eat noodles with chopsticks!

Traveler's Guide to Asian Culture, John Gottberg $12.95 (81-8) 356 pp.

John Gottberg, *Insight Guide* editor and co-author with Rick Steves of *Asia Through the Back Door,* has written for the traveler an accurate and enjoyable guide to the history and culture of this diverse continent. Sept. '88

Guide to Bus Touring in the U.S., Stuart Warren & Douglas Block $11.95 (95-8) 256 pp.

For many people, bus touring is the ideal, relaxed and comfortable way to see America. The author has had years of experience as a bus tour conductor and writes in-depth about every aspect of bus touring to help passengers get the most pleasure for their money. Sept. '88

Road & Track's Used Car Classics edited by Peter Bohr $12.95 (69-9) 272 pp.

Road & Track contributing editor Peter Bohr has compiled this collection of the magazine's "Used Car Classic" articles, updating them to include current market information. Over 70 makes and models of American, British, Italian, West German, Swedish and Japanese enthusiast cars built between 1953 and 1979 are featured.

Automotive Repair Manuals

Each JMP automotive manual gives clear step-by-step instructions, together with illustrations that show exactly how each system in the vehicle comes apart and goes back together. They tell everything a novice or experienced mechanic needs to know to perform periodic maintenance, tune-ups, troubleshooting and repair of the brake, fuel and emission control, electrical, cooling, clutch, transmission, driveline, steering and suspension systems, and even rebuild the engine.

How To Keep Your VW Alive $17.95 (50-8) 384 pp.
How To Keep Your VW Rabbit Alive $17.95 (47-8) 440 pp.
How To Keep Your Honda Car Alive $17.95 (55-9) 272 pp.
How To Keep Your Subaru Alive $17.95 (49-4) 464 pp.
How To Keep Your Toyota Pick-Up Alive $17.95 (89-3) 400 pp. April '88
How To Keep Your Datsun/Nissan Alive $22.95 (65-6) 544 pp.
How To Keep Your Honda ATC Alive $14.95 (45-1) 236 pp.

ITEM NO.			TITLE	EACH	QUAN.	TOTAL
		-				
		-				
		-				
		-				
		-				
		-				

Subtotals _____

Postage & handling (see ordering information)* _____

New Mexicans please add 5.625% tax _____

Total Amount Due _____

METHOD OF PAYMENT (circle one)   MC   VISA   AMEX   CHECK   MONEY ORDER

Credit Card Number

Expiration Date

Signature X _____
Required for Credit Card Purchases

Telephone: Office ( ) _____ Home ( ) _____

Name _____

Address _____

City _____ State _____ Zip _____

See reverse side for Ordering Information

ORDERING INFORMATION

Fill in the order blank. Be sure to add up all of the subtotals at the bottom of the order form, and give us the address whither your order will be whisked.

Postage & Handling

Your books will be sent to you via UPS (for U.S. destinations), and you will receive them in approximately 10 days from the time that we receive your order.

Include $2.75 for the first item ordered and add $.50 for each additional item to cover shipping and handling costs. UPS shipments to post office boxes take longer to arrive; if possible, please give us a street address.

For airmail within the U.S., enclose $4.00 per book for shipping and handling.

ALL FOREIGN ORDERS will be shipped surface rate. Please enclose $3.00 for the first item and $1.00 for each additional item. Please inquire for airmail rates.

Method of Payment

Your order may be paid by check, money order or credit card. We cannot be responsible for cash sent through the mail.

All payments must be in U.S. dollars drawn on a U.S. bank. Canadian postal money orders in U.S. dollars also accepted.

For VISA, Mastercard or American Express orders, use the order form or call (505) 982-4078. Books ordered on American Express cards can be shipped only to the billing address of the cardholder.

Sorry, no C.O.D.'s.

Residents of sunny New Mexico add 5.625% to the total.

Backorders

We will backorder all forthcoming and out-of-stock titles unless otherwise requested.

Address all orders and inquiries to:

JOHN MUIR PUBLICATIONS
P.O. Box 613
Santa Fe, NM 87504
(505) 982-4078

All prices subject to change without notice.